T0197243

KOSTIK

Chancing Execution, This Sixteen-Year-Old Escapes
to America from Czarist Russia by Himself and
Builds the American Dream

RICH KOPITUK

KOSTIK
CHANCING EXECUTION, THIS SIXTEEN-YEAR-OLD
ESCAPES TO AMERICA FROM CZARIST RUSSIA BY
HIMSELF AND BUILDS THE AMERICAN DREAM

iUniverse books may be ordered through booksellers or by contacting:

iUniverse
1663 Liberty Drive
Bloomington, IN 47403
www.iuniverse.com
1-800-Authors (1-800-288-4677)

ISBN: 978-1-5320-5135-7 (sc)
ISBN: 978-1-5320-5137-1 (hc)
ISBN: 978-1-5320-5136-4 (e)

Library of Congress Control Number: 2019900780

Print information available on the last page.

iUniverse rev. date: 02/26/2019

CONTENTS

CHAPTER ONE

Kostik Kopituk was born in 1894 in the village of Pinsk in Belarus. It was a village controlled by a member of the Czar's court (we will call him Lieutenant) who had fiefdom-style power over a small group of peasants. These people were totally dependent on the whims of this man who set the rules laid down under the land grant laws established by the Czar's government. These rules were quite restrictive allowing little or no opportunity for negotiation.

The domiciles were constructed in a manner specifying the amount of land on which each sat, the materials used and the size of the building. If one were to describe the structure, sparse would be an overstatement, for the building was more like a hut than a house. The barest of essentials was permitted. The ground was the floor, the roof was thatched, heat was provided by a fireplace which was also used for cooking, beds were made of straw and all were in one room. Of course, there was no indoor plumbing.

The village refrigerator was communal. A huge hole was dug in the ground in which were placed huge blocks of ice cut from the nearby river in winter by the men of the village. The ice was dragged to and carefully placed in the deep hole. Food staples were placed on the ice during the winter and covered with straw, ferns and other plants that maintained – for the most part – the ice in its frozen state throughout the short summer and fall. Fresh vegetables were grown by each of the families, but the types and amounts were governed.

Each hut was granted a garden space approximately three feet by fifty feet. At the end of the village, the first hut was given a second plot again of three feet by fifty feet, followed thereafter by the second hut's plot, etc. The reason for this manner of separation was because land ownership was considered power and no peasant was allowed power. Only the Czar's chosen were allowed that power, not all of the production from these gardens belonged to the peasants. A certain amount had to be given to the Czar's Lieutenant with pickings having been overseen by members of his guards.

There was one small bright spot for the Kopituk household, however. Kostik's father was looked upon favorably by the Lieutenant who gave him the responsibility for keeping the village cow. Each day the milk was given to all the villagers with the amount dependent upon the size of the family. Kostik's father also determined when the milk would be used to make butter.

This is the life into which Kostik was raised (Kostik anglicized to Constantine). The family was religious and espoused the Eastern Rite. Sunday church was an important facet of their lives as was education, meager as it was. Peasants were not allowed to attend school beyond the fourth grade. After leaving school, a young Russian peasant looked forward to work, some meaningful, some hard, menial labor or perhaps service in Czar's military. Kostik was hired by one of the Czar's construction companies where he became a bricklayer assistant. He was eleven years old.

During this period, there was a great deal of construction in Russia. Kostik was afforded the opportunity to see much of his country as he traveled to various construction sites. He was a hard worker and in a year he was promoted to a bricklayer apprentice. Soon after, he became a full-fledged bricklayer. Much of what he saw, such as the huge marble edifices that became the depots and terminals for the Czar's expanding railroads, would stay in his memory. These magnificent structures were markedly different from his village and the impoverished lifestyle of its people.

On one of his trips back to his village, he met a childhood friend, Itzahkh Cohen. To his shock, Kostik could not believe the proposition Itzahkh was suggesting: let's go to America. He didn't want an immediate answer, but he told Kostik to think about it quickly. Kostik said he would think about it but dismissed it in his happiness to be home for a short leave. He left without seeing Itzahkh again during that stay. A number of months later, now fifteen years old, Kostik returned home. The proposition had stayed with him, and he had revealed it to no one. At that time in Russia, any mention of leaving Russia brought dire consequences, possibly a visit from the special guard of the Czar – the KGB of the day, the Cossacks, which Russian peasantry deeply feared. Known for their brutality, no one wanted to have his criticism of the government reach Cossack ears. Kostik had once witnessed groups of peasants executed for such talk. So horrified by this scene, Kostik never again mentioned it in Russia. He still wanted to go to America.

As soon as he arrived in the village, he sought Itzahkh who told him that yes, he still was wanting to go to America. Kostik said he would get back to him this time. Parting from Itzahkh, Kostik waited for his brother-in-law to get home from his job as the supervisor of the Czar's lumber mill. He was the only man with whom Kostik could trust to discuss this; his father had died. Kostik's brother-in-law did not hesitate when he heard the proposition: GO!. He asked Kostik to look around. What did he see? What future did he see for himself as a bricklayer? What kind of life did he foresee? "If you can do it, Kostik, why do you hesitate?" Kostik left his brother-in-law and went after Itzahkh. They made their plans for the next day.

In Russia at that time, there was a very stringent law prohibiting leaving the country. Anyone caught talking about or actually attempting it could be sent to Siberia or executed. But there was an illicit, secret organization that was secretly established to help those willing to try. For a certain amount of rubles, the required papers, tickets and explicit instructions could be purchased. These instructions had to be followed without deviation. This was an "underground railroad" much like that used to help slaves in the United States escape the South during the War Between the States, but this was not to stay in the country but to escape it. Itzahkh and Kostik went to these people and were made ready to leave promptly when told to do so.

It would be a night of mixed emotions. The anticipation of several very life-changing events would be much for someone older and more experienced, but for a young boy who just celebrated his sixteenth birthday, the upcoming events were at once exhilarating and frightening. He would be leaving his family, leaving his country, and facing a dangerous escape fraught with extreme hazards. The night he repeatedly tossed and turned on his straw mattress.

Without a lot of explaining, Kostik told his mother he was going to spend the night with his sister and her husband. He was able to secretly pack his small valise, take it to the barn where the cow was stalled and hide it under the hay. He then slowly walked into the hut where his sister had prepared some of his favorite food: kapusta soup with black bread, hard salami, potatoes and vegetables. With his insides churning, he didn't eat much which his sister certainly understood. They talked about many things and he was asked two major questions: had he told mom what he was going to do and secondly, was he absolutely sure he was going to do what he was going to do. His answer to the first was no and to the second with no hesitation, a somewhat breathy yes. He would tell his mother in the morning.

Early the next morning, Kostik's mother came to the hut. She asked if they were going to church. They told her they didn't think so. As important as church was to her, she asked why they were not. Not getting a satisfactory answer, she then asked if they had fed the cow; no, they had not. She immediately turned and went to the barn, shaking her head and muttering dissatisfaction under her breath.

Not expecting what happened next, they remained seated, drinking their tea. In the barn, she picked up the pitch fork and plunged it into the hay to feed the cow, striking Kostik's suitcase. Picking it up, she returned hurriedly into the hut, asking Kostik why he had hidden the suitcase and where was he going. Rising and fighting to hold back tears, he told his mother he was going to America. Silence.

After what felt like minutes the barrage of questions came hard and fast, followed by weeping, wailing and gnashing of teeth from all four in the room. Kostik, crying loudly, looked at the clock and said he had to leave. Hugging and kissing the women, he hugged and kissed his brother-in-law, held both his hands, picked up his suitcase and shuffled and stumbled out the door. He did not look back. Had he done so, he would've seen his brother-in-law holding his mother up as she cried hysterically, wringing her hands. He heard the crying, increased his pace to get out of earshot and walked briskly to meet Itzahkh.

As the two met, they stopped and faced each other, neither boy saying anything. Each looked down at the ground, looked past each other, and then looked straight into each other's eyes. Itzahkh said that it was time to catch a train.

CHAPTER TWO

Their voices returned as they walked to the train station. Both had experienced the same family departure which brought tears to both boys. As they approached the station, they stopped to check that each had all the papers and tickets they were supposed to have. They placed the train tickets in their pockets but kept the other papers and ship tickets hidden — hopefully — under their clothing.

As the train came to a stop, they rushed inside to make certain they could get two seats together on the right side of the car nearest to the door in which they were riding. The conductor took their tickets and asked them where they were going so early in the morning. Passing pleasantries, the conductor moved on. Somewhat relieved, the boys looked at each other, hoping their answers were acceptable and further hoping their nervousness didn't show.

As the train was getting closer to the next station, Kostik looked over at Itzahkh and told him he had better sit on his hands or put them in his pockets. Itzahkh looked at Kostik and asked why. "Because they're shaking," Kostik told him. Itzahkh looked at his hands to see they definitely were! He put them in his pockets and told Kostik to stop looking at everybody as if something were going to happen. Kostik stopped, not realizing he had been doing that. There was no point in looking guilty! They quickly reviewed — almost in a whisper — what they had been instructed and said a fast prayer that they would come out safely.

The boys could feel the engineer applying the brakes to slow the train as it approached the station, was on the left side of the train and a huge forest was to the right. The train slowed to a crawl. The boys took their valises, stood up and walked to the door. Several passengers called out that the boys must be in a hurry to meet their girlfriends. With forced smiles, they acknowledged that was so and they couldn't wait. Once on the car's platform, they turned to the right and jumped off the train. They hit the ground and rolled as they had been taught; they saw the Cossacks! Some were running, firing their rifles. Others, with drawn sabers, were on horseback. The boys ran into the woods, bullets whizzing past them! The Cossacks followed but the trees were so thick, they were fairly well protected from the bullets. They ran fast, running out of breath but forcing themselves to go on. When are those Cossacks going to stop each asked himself. At last they did but the boys did not stop until they came to a clearing at the far edge of the forest. When they reached the clearing, they leaned against a tree to get their wheezing under control. They looked out into the clearing, hoping to see what they were told would be waiting for them – a huge haywagon pulled by eight horses.

Several other young men were running toward the wagon and those who had already reached it were crawling over the tailgate and burrowing under the hay. The two boys started running to the wagon to do the same thing.

Waiting under the hay for what seemed an eternity, Kostik heard the rifle shots echoing through the forest. He would learn later that the farmer was to have had twenty young men on the wagon; only sixteen made it. The fate of the missing four became a subject of discussion at the next stop.

At last, all sixteen finally felt the wagon begin to roll. They heard the farmer vocally prodding the four teams to pull the huge heavy hay-laden wagon as fast as he dared. It would be several hours to the next destination. Dusk was beginning to fall as the teams pulled into the yard where the young men would spend the night in a barn. They eased out of the hay, several coughing, several sneezing, trying to clear their parched throats and hay dust dried noses.

Within an hour after their arrival, a new farmer entered the barn, followed by his wife and two pretty daughters. Each was carrying canisters of food. Placing these on benches, they left to soon return with plates, utensils and drinks of cold water and hot tea. The meal consisted of thick barley soup and black bread which the men unashamedly devoured. As quickly as the canisters were emptied, they were refilled. During the meal, each man introduced himself and told of his background. Some came from farming, some from factories and lumber jobs; all were looking forward to the new life in America. Believing they were of like mind, they began speaking timidly, then harshly of the life they and their families had endured under the Czar. But strangely, the Czar was not spoken of derogatorily.

Throughout Russia he was, in many peasant circles, spoken of with reverence. The same could not be said of the Czarina. Of German heritage, she was looked upon as anti-Russian, and as imposing harsh German rule and culture on the Russians. (Her favoring Germany became very evident during World War I when she ordered sticks, brooms and other useless items to be sent as weapons to the Russian soldiers fighting the Germans).

Many of the sixteen young men related stories of starvation and beatings members of their families suffered, and the severe treatment they themselves had received, mostly from the Cossacks. They had learned not to trust any neighbor or friend. Anyone hearing anti-government talk could take matters into his own hands to show that he was still loyal to the Czar. Although it was a word not readily used in their lifetime, all mentioned how it was going to feel to have freedom for the first time in their lives. Several tried to define it and, with difficulty, the idea of what freedom was to them was as pure as any depiction that might have been given by the most learned of men.

Soon the talk – speculation – focused on the four young men who had not made it to the wagon. What would be their fate or, actually, what may have already been their fate? All claimed to know of the beheadings carried out by the Cossacks, several claiming to have witnessed those executions, weeping as they told of it. Others told of severe beatings, four of whom had been recipients themselves of the Cossacks' horrifying treatment. Why they were released and not sent to Siberia they did not know, but laughingly, how grateful they had not been.

The events of that day began taking their toll on the young men as eyelids became heavy. The beckoning of the straw on which they were sitting was too much to resist as one by one each fell backwards, falling rapidly into very deep sleep. It wasn't long before the cacophonous symphony of snoring resounded off the walls of the barn, but sleep was a luxury short-lived. A timetable had been established that permitted little or no deviation. The farmer again entered the barn, raucously arousing the men. Breakfast was served; thick barley soup and black bread again was the meal.

With suitcases in hand, they left the barn. Awaiting them was the sound of hoofed-feet stomping the ground, and whinnying from another team of eight horses hitched to another monster of a hay wagon. As soon as he had hurried the last man under the hay, this second farmer bade farewell to his family, climbed onto the driver's perch and set the horses moving. There were several nightly stops before the next final Russian destination; each next day's travel was conducted by a new farmer and wagon.

The Russian journey ended a short distance from the border of Russia and Germany. The farmer stopped his team behind a hill that hid his wagon from view from the border patrolled by Russian and German guards. The farmer jumped down from the wagon and walked over the hill. Two Russian guards and their officer met him, each guard holding his rifle at the ready, the officer his pistol. Speaking softly, the farmer showed them he was no danger to them. From his pocket, he pulled a goodly sum of Russian rubles which he gave the officer and told them what he wanted them to do. They did as they were asked: take a walk. Next, he went to the Germans with the same strategy. They, too, took a walk. It seems that this was something not unfamiliar to both nationalities standing border patrol.

CHAPTER THREE

The last and most grueling aspect of the land trip now faced the men. They had only a few weeks to get to Le Havre, France without mobile transportation. Not to attract attention to themselves, some chose partners, some struck out singly. Furthermore, since they were in a foreign country and not speaking the language, they took great care to have stories ready to explore why they were there and what their destination was and why they were travelling. Many suggestions were given by the underground; they had to remember word for word the story each would tell when he encountered any of the local population with whom he might be able to converse. Kostik and Itzahkh rehearsed theirs over and over as they began their trek. The maps they were given were all the same which meant the men were relatively short distances apart but, hopefully not that close to attract attention. They walked fast, slow, ran when they could, sought out woods – whatever was necessary. Food was definitely a problem; many would probably lose a great deal of weight. They relied heavily on locals, using sign language to indicate they would work for food; however, there wasn't much time they could spend at any one stop. Some locals offered shelter in an outbuilding for a night. When none was available, Kostik and Itzahkh slept under bridges, taking turns staying awake to watch for danger from dogs and wolves. Of course, they had no firearms and relied on large sticks and rocks, hoping their aim was sufficiently on the mark when it became necessary. Fortunately for the two of them, their weapons never had to be put to use.

When they were about a day from where the ship was docked, they detected a smell which was not in the least offensive, but neither could determine what it was. In fact, it was quite pleasant – salt sea air! Why had the temperature seemed to drop? Suddenly they heard a train whistle! They ran toward the sound which was coming from the other side of a hill that blocked their view. Running over the hill, they looked down on a slow-moving train that had several boxcars with open doors. Each of the boys inaudible thinking was of like mind. Should we take the chance? Is it moving slow enough to jump on? Is it going where we want to go? What if it speeds up so we can't get off if we want? Well, we have jumped from one train. What if we're spotted? They might shoot at us. No, there are no Cossacks here. The people so far have been friendly. Yes? No? As if they could sense each other's thoughts, they ran to the train which was going in the direction they wanted to go. Choosing a box car, they ran alongside it, threw their valises through the open door, timed their jump and leaped onto the car. To their surprise, four others of their group were already on board and helped pull them into the car.

After a short time, the train began to slow even more. They carefully looked out and saw in the distance what appeared to be a building. Could this be Le Havre. It had to be. They hugged each other and slapped each other on the back. Still unsure, but believing it was Le Havre, they let out whoops of joy, jumping up and down and dancing around the car. It had to be Le Havre! It was!

The train slowed to a speed to allow them to leap from it. Their valises were thrown out first, followed by six not-so-graceful leaping bodies in a variety of configurations. Thankfully, no major injuries resulted but one who forgot his rolling instructions sprained his ankle. This was not what the boys needed right now, but they took turns piggy-backing, shoulder leaning, and carrying the injured one. As they entered what appeared to be the center of the city, they encountered peddlers with food, drink, trinkets, toys and many more things on which travelers could waste their money. Because Le Havre was the destination for many people who had preceded them, some of the local peddlers had picked up some words in many different languages. The boys heard one peddler speaking in very broken Russian about immigrants who were willing to chance the consequences of crossing the Atlantic. The boys approached the Russian who was conversing with the peddler. They did so hesitantly because they were told by the underground that the Czarina had sent German soldiers to capture and return Russian escapees. They listened to the man speak Russian and recognized a German accent. Quickly the boys split up except the three who were involved with the ankle problem. They were surrounded before they knew what was happening.

The three who got away from the Germans remained within sight of each other. Kostik gestured to Itzahkh that he was going to ask a peddler which way it was to get to the ships. Itzahkh nodded in understanding and watched his friend approach a shopkeeper. Sign language worked in this case because neither spoke any of the other's language. Kostik bowed in the Russian way of thanks, stepped back, gestured to Itzahkh and walked in the direction the shopkeeper had pointed. Itzahkh and the other boy caught up with Kostik and the three now hurried toward the docks.

Yet apprehensive because of what had befallen the other three, they glanced left, they glanced right so very furtively. Kostik told the other two not to do what he was going to do; it would draw too much attention were all three to look back. Kostik quickly looked. With a big smile, Kostik slapped Itzahkh on the shoulder and told both boys to look back. They most certainly were being followed: followed by men, women, children, women carrying babies, all with suitcases, all apparently bent on getting to exactly where the three boys were going.

НОВАЯ КАРТА
РОССIЙСКОЙ
ИМПЕРIИ
раздѣленная на
Намѣстничества
Сочиненная
1786

CHAPTER FOUR

As they entered the dock area, they spotted their ship. They couldn't miss it. Hundreds of people lined the rail, packed the gangways up to the main deck and formed a snake-like line leading to the gangway. Itzahkh quietly said to the other two that so many of the men and women, and even the young girls appeared very heavy. They learned for good reason why they appeared so heavy. Almost all had several pants, shirts and jackets on, several long undergarments, dresses and coats. There was no space in the suitcases for the needed additional clothing. The easiest solution was to wear it.

Once on board, the people were herded into groups. One by one these groups were led below a number of decks to "steerage class"- the cheapest fare that bought them accommodation with minimal conveniences and very minimal comfort. It wasn't long before the body heat factor inside and summer heat outside heating up the steel sides of the ship contributed greatly to stomach illness of the worst kind in such a crowded condition. It couldn't be called sea-sickness because they weren't yet at sea. The smell was horrendous and still the people pressed into the spaces. Escape to the top deck was virtually impossible: all ladders were occupied by passengers coming down. There was no upward movement at all. The ship's crew knew very well what would happen: they were nowhere to be seen.

Several hours of this hellish existence finally came to a relative close when the ladder was cleared for up and down travel. The three boys, their clothing vomit-splattered, their bodies fatigued, sweaty and clammy, simultaneously, began clambering up the ladders to get out of the hole. Once on the main deck, they filled their lungs with what most people take for granted: sweet-smelling, life-giving air. They found rags and water with which they were able to wash themselves and their clothing. Feeling halfway human, they didn't go below deck that night. It was warm enough to remain out and sleep in the open.

The three slept deeply. Their minds told them they were now safe. The Czar and Czarina could no longer interfere with their lives, could no longer pose threats to their destiny. Destiny was now theirs. But they had a rude awakening in the morning: many voices were yelling as the lines tethering the ship were to let go, and the gangway was removed. The ship began to vibrate as her propeller grabbed the water to make her move, tugboats' whistles blared various signals to each other and a cacophony of sound resonated throughout the harbor. The three young boys were in awe of what was taking place. A ship carrying hundreds of humanity plied her way with whistle screaming through the crisscrossing vessels around her.

CHAPTER FIVE

Other than the anticipation of reaching the country that promised much, the Atlantic crossing was uneventful. The ship was a huge attraction to the boys, capturing hours of their days as they explored the vessel from the forward most part of the main deck to the farthest rear, from the top of the structure from which the ship was controlled down into the engine room, both of which were off limits to the passengers; however, the Captain for unknown reasons, took a liking to the three boys. Perhaps it was their curiosity that reminded him of his first time on a huge ship. He took the boys into his care for the entire crossing, giving them as much of his time as he could spare. He actually led them into the pilot house from where the ship was steered and from where the engine and rudder were given their commands. Each of the boys was given an opportunity to steer the ship. The Captain was able through the ever-called-upon sign language and finger pointing to figures on the compass which was directly in front of the helm, to order the boys each in his turn at the wheel to move the ship several degrees to the right, to the left and back to the course they had been on. Did this put thoughts of becoming a ship's captain into the head of each? Time would tell.

The ship's whistle woke the boys. They looked forward, broad smiles breaking their sleep-worn faces. There was America directly ahead. The ship was slowing, quietly gliding into New York harbor. Soon hatches were opened, and people wishing to get off the ship as quickly as possible streamed from them. Many ran to the rail to see this tall statue of a woman holding a torch in one hand, a book in the other. She was dressed in a long gown and wore a crown on her head. Some had heard of her; many had not. They all would learn of America's liberty, statue of and reality, as time went on.

The ship turned to her berthing space and at last was tied to the dock. The gangway was set in place and the passengers were instructed to disembark. They were directed to a ferry boat that would take them to Ellis Island. There they would be fed, seated on backless benches at tables some twenty feet long. To some, the food was strange and unfamiliar. As hungry as most were, it really didn't matter how strange and unfamiliar. It was food.

After eating, the immigrants were directed toward examining rooms where they underwent the most rudimentary – and unsanitary – physical examination. At last, it was time to talk with an immigration officer. This was where a new life might begin. This was also where a heart might be broken. Most would be allowed to stay in America; however, some would not for a multitude of reasons: diseases, lack of financial resources, no specific destination, no sponsors. The boys had passed their physicals and had been counseled well in Russia. They had been told questions the immigration officers would ask and had rehearsed them with a variety of answers.

From the examination room, they were told where to go to get to a Russian speaking officer. Kostik was the first called to sit at a table in front of one of the officers who would ask a myriad of questions and listen carefully for correct or at least very satisfactory answers.

"Where in Russia are you from?"

"Pinsk."

"Can you read and write?"

"Yes."

"Have you ever been in jail?"

"No."

"What work did you do in the old country."

"I was a bricklayer."

"Will you do this in America?"

"That's what I was hoping to do, yes."

"Is someone meeting you."

"Yes."

"Who?"

"A man from my village who came to America two years ago."

"Do you have papers?"

"Yes."

"Let me see those. Where did you get these papers?"

"Why? Is something wrong?"

(Kostik began to tremble. His hands grew clammy. He began to feel drops of perspiration sliding down his back. He swallowed hard but there was nothing to swallow. His mouth had grown as dry as some of the deserts he had crossed in Russia in his travels to construction sites.)

"No, these papers are filled out correctly. Where do you want to go if you are permitted to stay?"

"Elizabethport, New Jersey."

"Why? Is your sponsor there?"

"Yes."

"Who is your sponsor?"

"Andy Gorelick."

"Is he a relative? I didn't think you are Jewish."

"By marriage."

(The agent hesitated. He looked directly at Kostik. Kostik felt beads of perspiration form on his forehead and under his eyes. When the agent picked up the papers, straightened them and turned to look on the table behind him, Kostik wiped his forehead and eyes with the rag he brought with him from the ship.)

"How much money do you have, Kostik?"

(This was the first time the agent called him by name since having been called to come to the table. What did that mean?)

"I have five rubles."

"Give them to me. I have something for you."

(The agent gave Kostik a stick of hard salami and several slices of black bread wrapped in newspaper."

The agent had Kostik stand up. He hung two signs around his neck, one on his chest, the other on his back. The first said, "Please direct me to the Jersey Central Ferry." The second said, "Conductor, please let me off at Elizabethport, New Jersey." The agent gave Kostik instructions, shook his hand and welcomed him to America. Kostik turned and saw Itzahkh. They came together, said goodbye, hugged for long seconds and parted. They would never again see each other and neither saw the other boy. Whether Itzahkh saw him after Kostik left the building, Kostik would never know.

CHAPTER SIX

Kostik left the building and saw where he was to get onto the ferry boat that would take him to the lower end of Manhattan. He was told it would be a long walk up the island to the Jersey Central Ferry but that there really was no rush. The trains – one of which he would have to catch on the New Jersey side – ran frequently throughout the day so if he missed one, another would be leaving in a short while.

The boat ride was relatively short. Kostik looked back at Ellis Island and the tall statue of that lady in the harbor. He crossed himself in the Eastern Rite crossing the opposite of the Roman Catholic sign of the cross. As he did that, he thanked God for his good fortune so far, asked for His continued blessing, asked that He bless his family and give a special blessing to Matka (mother). The boat reached the dock with a jarring hit. The young man in charge apparently didn't know – or hadn't learned yet – how to slow and stop the boat. Kostik jumped from the boat and walked to what appeared to be a main street. He walked toward the first man he saw, pointing to the Jersey Central Ferry sign on his chest. The man smiled and pointed in the direction Kostik should go.

Some time passed and Kostik began to feel hungry. After all, the excitement of the past few hours he had not thought much about food but did now. He stopped, sat down on the lowest step of one of the buildings, took out the salami and black bread and began to eat. It wasn't long before he was joined by several visitors: two seagulls, which in turn were scared away by two cats which in turn were scared away by a medium sized dog. The dog seemed friendly enough so Kostik threw part of his food to the dog, stood up, stretched and started walking again in the direction he had been told. Periodically, he pointed to his sign as he approached other people. They reassured him his direction was correct.

Without realizing it, his next sign-pointing turned out to be his last. The middle-aged woman he was approaching directed him to turn to his left. There in front of him was the river, the dock and a fairly good-sized vessel tied to it. The man standing at the entrance to the ferry stopped Kostik, showed him a ticket. Kostik shrugged his shoulders in the international sign of "So, what now?" The man pulled some money out of his pocket. Kostik got the message. He reached into his pocket for the change that he had been given when the agent on Ellis Island took his rubles for the salami and black bread. Kostik held what he had out to the man who took what he needed, gave back the remainder and gestured him aboard. As the ferry crossed the Hudson River to the New Jersey side, Kostik slipped the front sign off and seeing no place to dispose of it, threw it into the river. He watched as the little sign was hit by the ferry's bow wave and followed it as it floated down the side of the ferry and finally disappeared. Kostik sat down, placed his valise between his legs and looked out at the next stop of his adventure – New Jersey. The boat's whistle sounded. The ferry was at the Jersey side of the river.

The bow gate was swung open by one of the boat's crew who motioned for the passengers to leave the ferry. Kostik looked back one more time at New York City, bent down to pick up his faithful traveling companion valise, left the rail against which he had been leaning and followed the crowd off the vessel. Once more he looked down to be sure that his "Conductor, please let me off at Elizabethport, New Jersey" sign was clearly straight and visible. As he approached the several waiting trains, he looked for someone whom he thought might be able to direct him to the correct train. Spotting a man dressed in some sort of uniform, he walked to the man and pointed to the sign on his chest. Smiling, the man who was a conductor put his hand on Kostik's shoulder, turned him and walked with him to the train he was to board. As they came to the steps of the car, Kostik placed his valise on the ground, extended his hand and with a slight European gesture of a boy, grasped the conductor's hand with both of his own, turned and boarded the car. Finding a seat next to a window, Kostik sat and looked out, again placing his valise between his legs. There was nothing for him to see except another train parked next to his. He leaned back, closed his eyes and took a very deep breath and released it slowly. He felt his eyes welling up, closed his eyes tight and pressed the heels of his hands against them and wiped the tears before they dripped down his face. Embarrassed, he turned quickly toward the window so as not to be seen by anyone who might sit down next to him. Unfortunately, a person in the next train unexpectedly was looking at him which did nothing to mitigate his embarrassment. He turned, faced forward and wiped his eyes with the back and heel of his right hand. He took another deep breath just as the train lurched. Under his breath he thanked God for his having safely reached New Jersey.

Kostik felt the seat move as a man sat down next to him. He turned, both men nodded in acknowledgment. The man spoke a greeting in English and all Kostik could do was shrug his shoulders to let the man know he didn't understand. He pointed to the sign on his chest to which the man smiled in recognition. Kostik turned again to look out the window. It wasn't a pretty landscape that he saw: somewhat dilapidated houses and small smoke belching factories. He faced forward again. He leaned back and closed his eyes. A change in sound snapped his eyes open. The train was on a bridge crossing the Passaic River. He didn't know it, but it wouldn't be much longer.

The train slowed and the conductor who had helped him motioned for him to come out of the seat and pointed to the door. The train stopped, the conductor waved and Kostik stepped down from the train. As he looked at the train station, he caught his breath. This ramshackled little building was an absolute shock to him. After several years of working on the huge marble edifices that were the Czar's train stations in Russia, how could this be America? Is this the America he had heard so much about? Russia's trains were a major significance in the lives of the people. Did America not appreciate trains? Were America's trains considered so much junk? In his mind, because of this aspect of American life based on his experience, had he made a monumental mistake in leaving his country? Well, he thought, he was here. There's no going back now. He would see what was to happen he told himself. This was it. He was in America. That was all there was to it. What now?

CHAPTER SEVEN

He walked around the station building behind which was an open field. Two boys were playing catch, saw him and walked to meet him. He looked like no one either knew, saw the little valise and being familiar with what was happening in America at the time and particularly in their community, they assumed he was another newly arrived immigrant. He looked and was dressed much like the people who lived in Elizabethport, an Eastern European melting pot. The city had been settled by Polish, Russians, Ukrainians, Slavs, Czechoslovaks and Yugoslavs. They spoke to him in Polish. He answered in Russian which they recognized. The boys looked around and pointed to a man walking across the street. They motioned to Kostik to come with them. One of the boys took Kostik by the hand and again pointed to the man whom they apparently knew; they called to him. The man turned and walked to meet them. He, too, recognized that the man with the boys was a new immigrant.

The man was Russian and spoke to Kostik. Overwhelmed, Kostik broke down. The man fully understood. He wrapped his arms around Kostik, hugged him and let him get it out of his system. After several minutes, Kostik calmed himself. The man pulled a blue rag from his rear pocket and handed it to Kostik. As Kostik wiped his eyes and face, the two Polish boys patted his shoulders and said with one of the few words of Russian they knew, goodbye.

"What is your name?" the man said.

"Kostik Kopituk. I am from Pinsk."

"You are very young. How old are you?"

"Sixteen."

"Where are your mother and father?"

"Mother in Russia. Father died several years ago."

"You came by yourself?" the man asked incredulously.

"Yes, with a friend."

"A friend? Where is he?"

"We left each other on Ellis Island."

"Do you know where he was going?"

"Yes, he was meeting some people in New York."

"How did you know him?"

"He lived in my village. He was the one who suggested we go to America."

"Do you have anyone here? Do you have a place to stay?"

"There's a man from my village who came here two years ago. I'll have to find him. No, I don't have a place to stay."

"Come, I'll take you to a woman, Mrs. Nevar, who takes people in. She may have room for one more. As we walk, tell me how you got out of Russia. You sneaked out, didn't you?"

As they walked Kostik related the whole harrowing tale of the escape from Russia and the trek across Russia, Germany and France.

"Oh, I didn't tell you my name, it is Ivan Petrovich," said the Russian man.

"I'm sorry I didn't ask you," replied Kostik. "Where are you from?" he asked.

"I am from Minsk."

"Did you do as I did to get out?"

"Yes, but my escape was not as bad as yours. I don't know why we didn't have the Cossacks after us like you, and our border crossing was easy. There were no guards where our advisers told us to cross. Well, here we are at Mrs. Nevar's house. She is a very lovely person. I stayed with her when I first came until I got a job and was able to move out to a less crowded house. Come, I will introduce you."

"Thank you, Ivan. I appreciate you taking your time to help me."

"No thanks is necessary, my friend. I know what you are feeling. You are not alone in your thoughts. Everyone has the same scary thoughts."

Ivan and Kostik climbed the steps to the porch and knocked on the door. After a short wait, Ivan knocked again just as the door opened. Standing before them was a short stout woman in her long multicolored house dress, a woman in her late forties with a slightly wrinkled face and a warm smile.

"Ah, Ivan, you have brought me another one...but, he is so young," she exclaimed. "Come in, both of you."

"Welcome young man," she said as she stepped back to let them pass.

"Eugenia, this is Kostik Kopituk from Pinsk. Kostik, this is Eugenia Nevar," said Ivan.

Kostik bowed as he reached for her outstretched hand.

"I am happy to be here," he said.

"I am happy to see you, Kostik. Come into the kitchen. I have some hot water on the stove, and we will have some tea."

Kostik and Ivan followed her to the kitchen where she pointed to two chairs for them to sit down. As they sat, she put a cup, saucer and spoon in front of each of them and placed a bowl of sugar cubes and a bowl of tea leaves between them. Ivan took his spoon and dipped some tea leaves into his cup. Kostik did the same. Eugenia poured the hot water into their cups and told them to let the tea set.

"You came through Ellis Island?" Eugenia asked Kostik.

"Yes," he answered.

"Where did you catch the ship?"

"Le Havre. I arrived three days ago and today I was taken to New York City and walked all the way to where I got to a ferry that took me across the river to the train," Kostik said.

"I think the tea might be ready. Let's drink a welcome to America drink," Eugenia suggested.

The three poured their tea into their saucers, lifted the saucers, placed their thumbs and three fingers under the saucer, tilted them and drank their tea.

"Well, Kostik, Ivan stayed with me for a couple of months, and I guess he brought you here for the same reason he came here. Would you like to stay here?" said Eugenia.

"Yes, if you will let me," Kostik replied.

"Yes, I have room for one more. I have two other men staying here. They are very nice, and I think you will get along good with them, though I think they are older than you. How old are you? You look very young."

"I am sixteen. Hold old are they?" Kostik asked.

"Evgeny is twenty-six and Timofe is twenty-nine. They have been here for about six months.

Each of them have jobs. One works in the daytime and one works in the night which will work out well for you since there is only one bed. You will arrange the sleeping time with them."

Eugenia explained. "Come, let me show you the room. You come, too, Ivan. I'm sure you will have some memories of this."

"Of course, Eugenia. I remember very good how this works," said Ivan with a chuckle.

The three of them went to the room. Surprisingly, it was very neat and well kept. The bed was not empty. Evgeny, who worked nights was asleep. He heard the slight rustling, opened one eye, raised his head, said nothing, turned over and went back to sleep. The three left the bedroom.

Back in the kitchen, Eugenia poured more hot water in their cups and the three sat again.

"I have some rules, Kostik. First, there is to be no drinking. You know, I'm certain, that you know the kind of drinking I am talking about. Do you smoke? If you do, you can't smoke in the house, you have to go outside."

"I don't drink, and I don't smoke," Kostik replied.

"Good," answered Eugenia. "Now, I serve three meals a day. I wash clothes once a week. I keep separate baskets for each person. I expect you to keep clean, so you must take a bath once a week. This is a big house, so I will ask you once in a while to help me do some housework like sweep the floors, sweep the porch, make small little repairs when something might need to be fixed. Also, outside the sidewalk needs to be swept once in a while. Also, outside the windows need to be washed once in a while but not so many times. Does all of this sound all right with you, Kostik?"

"Yes, it sounds all right with me," Kostik answered.

"Now, do you have money?" Eugenia asked.

"Yes, I have, but is there some place that will take my Russian money and give me American money for it?" Kostik asked. "I gave five rubles to the officer on Ellis Island, and he gave me some black bread and salami and two American dollars and several coins, but I have more Russian money."

Ivan spoke. "I can take you where you can get American money."

"Mrs. Nevar, all of what you do, you don't do for free. What do you charge to stay here?" Kostik asked.

"I charge twenty-five cents a week, but you are going to have to get a job and go to work. I will help you with the cost, but I expect you to start looking for work right away. Ivan, can you help him?"

"Yes, I can show him around. Where I work they are not hiring but there are places that have signs on their doors looking for workers. I'll show you. When do you want to start? You told me you were a bricklayer in Russia. I don't know of any place looking for bricklayers, but we can ask around."

"I don't like to say it, but I am a little tired right now. I would like to go to sleep. What about tomorrow morning. Can you do it with me tomorrow?"

"Yes, I can. I have to go now, but I will come by first thing tomorrow morning. Will you be ready?"

"I will be ready."

CHAPTER EIGHT

Kostik went into the bedroom and as quietly as he could, opened his valise, removed his night clothes and changed from his shirt and pants. Evgeny was still asleep and was far enough on one side of the bed allowing room for Kostik to get on the other side. He quickly fell into a deep sleep. He slept so hard that he heard neither Evgeny get out of bed to go to work nor the other man get in the bed to sleep.

It was six o'clock in the morning when the other man woke, got out of bed and dressed to go into the kitchen for breakfast. Eugenia asked the man if Kostik was awake. Being told no, she went in to wake him. She wanted him ready for Ivan.

Kostik quickly dressed and went into the kitchen. Eugenia greeted him.

"Kostik, this is Timofe. Timofe, this is Kostik. He is from Pinsk, and Ivan brought him here yesterday."

"Hello, Kostik. I am from Odessa in the Ukraine. I came to America three months ago," said Timofe. Eugenia tells me you are going with Ivan to look for work. What did you do in Russia?"

"I was a bricklayer. Do you know of any company that would give me work?"

"There is building going on, but I don't know anyone who is working on any of those jobs."

The two young men talked while eating the breakfast Eugenia had prepared. Shortly, Timofe rose, said goodbye and left. Kostik helped Eugenia remove the dishes from the table and placed them in the sink. The back door opened, and Ivan entered the kitchen. He asked Kostik if he were ready to go look for work.

They said goodbye to Eugenia and left the house. As they walked to where stores and small factories were, they talked of their lives in Russia. Though both had lived sparsely, Ivan's life had been harder than Kostik's. Since Kostik's father had been chosen by the Czar's Lieutenant to be the village's leader, his family had a few more privileges than the other villagers. Ivan had gotten into trouble several times which almost prevented his being allowed into America. But the guards at Ellis Island seemed to have taken a liking to him and waived the rule blocking his entrance into America.

They finally walked into the area where there were businesses. They walked past several businesses until they came to one that had a "Help Wanted" sign on the door, but this sign had another sign below it: "WORK FOR GERMANS ONLY." The "Help Wanted" sign on another building stated "RUSSIANS AND UKRANIANS DO NOT COME IN." Another stated "WORK FOR POLISH ONLY." Many businesses had similarly worded signs, reading who of the various ethnic groups need not apply; very few did not have such signs.

Kostik finally looked at Ivan and asked why was there so much dislike for so many people.

"I never thought America had so much of this kind of feeling," said Kostik.

"This is the first time for many of these business owners who are not used to working with so many not of their own kind," answered Ivan. "Remember, Kostik, that all the men you worked with were Russian. Did you work with Germans? Did you work with Italians, French?"

"No. Well, some Germans. They were good workers, but mostly Russians. We ate Russian food. We spoke Russian. We knew stories that told of Russian people."

"So, there you have it, Kostik. It may take generations for America to become a country of one people. Only time will tell," said Ivan.

"Well, I want to become an American," said Kostik strongly.

"And what is that, Kostik?" asked Ivan, his brow furrowed.

"I guess I don't know yet, Ivan. I don't know what it is to be an American, but there has to be an answer for that."

CHAPTER NINE

They continued walking around the business area. They came upon a big building from which came a strange, but strong smell which Ivan recognized. The building had only one sign: "HELP WANTED."

"I am told this business is called a tannishery," said Ivan. Ivan did not know the word tannery.

"A what?" asked Kostik.

"A tannishing place. They do something with cow skins. They make some kind of clothes with them," answered Ivan.

"Like coats?" questioned Kostik.

"I guess so. Anyhow, they are looking for help. Do you want to go in?"

"I might as well. It looks like they will hire anybody," said Kostik.

They entered the building and were met by a big man in a leather apron. The man smiled and said one questioning word: Russian? They both answered the Russian "yes" - da. He held up his hand for them to wait.

The man turned and called to another man. "Hey, Sergei, come here," he called. Sergei spoke Russian and fairly good American. Sergei came running. With strong Russian accent, the man asked what was wrong.

"Nothing wrong, Sergei. Ask these two what they want. They're Russian." Sergei asked, and Ivan answered, "This is Kostik. He just came in from Ellis and is looking for work."

Sergei spoke to the first man who wanted to know what Kostik knew about tanning.

Kostik told them that he knew nothing about tanning. He offered and admitted he really did not know what the word meant. Sergei laughed and slapped Kostik on his shoulder. Kostik smiled nervously.

31

"My name is Smitty, I am the foreman here. Tell them what I said, Sergei, and explain what a foreman is. Then ask them if they want to work."

Sergei repeated what Smitty had said and asked the question. Kostik answered that he wanted to work but that Ivan already had a job. He further stated he knew nothing of tanning and is there someone who would teach him.

Sergei told Smitty who nodded and had Sergei take Kostik to a table and had him sit. Smitty took Sergei aside. "This young man looks like he might be good. But, I don't want to put him in any tanning process yet. Let's see how much he is really willing to work. We need another worker to pick up the scraps, clean the floors and take it all out to the company's garbage pit. Put him with the German and have him go around with him for a day or two. We'll see what happens."

Sergei introduced Kostik to German, the German. German had learned some Russian in the time he had been working at the tannery. On the other hand, Kostik had learned some of the German language from the construction workers in Russia who had come from Germany to work on the Czar's construction crew on which Kostik worked.

"German, wie lange hast du hier arbeite," Kostik asked in broken German.

"Ich arbeite zwei jahren," German answered. "Zer gut."

"I talk American some, Kostik. Please talk to me in American. I must learn the words," said German.

Kostik did not understand German so he just nodded. German realized that neither he nor Kostik understood each other.

Kostik received his first pay at the end of the week. He was paid one dollar. He walked quickly to Eugenia's house and showed her the dollar.

"Do you want to pay me for the week, Kostik?" asked Eugenia.

"Yes, please take what I owe you."

"I told you that I charge twenty-five cents for room, food and also ask that you help with some work around the house. Without asking, I have already watched you wash dishes, sweep the floors and porch. I am surprised. You are not afraid to work."

"Our life in Russia was not easy. I learned a simple rule – you want to eat, then you work.

Don't expect handouts. Now, one dollar is not much for a week's work from what I can see, but I will prove my worth to this man who hired me, and when I do, I believe he will give me more."

"Kostik, you will work for this man for a while, but I see you doing more than working in a tanning factory. You are young in years, but much older in life already. I see that in you. You are a different person, a different young person. I think you see things different from what Ivan, Timofe or Sergei see. Already, I can see that if I ever have a son, I would like him to be like you."

At that, Kostik smiled, awkwardly approached Eugenia and hugged her. She put her arms around the young man and hugged him tightly. She then backed away, held out her hand and they shook hands.

"Now, what are you going to do with the seventy-five cents you have left?" Eugenia asked.

"He's going out with us," Timofe broke in.

"Yes, we are going to go to Timoshenko's Bar," Sergei said. "We will introduce him to how we have fun on Saturday nights in America."

"You be careful with him, Timofe and Sergei. He is still very young and is not used to the kind of men - and girls, for that matter – that go in those places," Eugenia said very sternly.

"Oh, he will be fine. I'm sure in Russia he saw plenty in those places where the Czar's buildings were being built, didn't you, Kostik?"

"I saw some things, yes; but, I didn't like a lot of what went on." They laughed, but Kostik did not.

"See? See, you men. He is not stupid." Eugenia stood her ground, arms folded over her chest, rocking back and forth on her heels.

"Well, we go. Come, Kostik. We go to have laughter, drink a little bit, dance with the girls.

Who knows, you might get kissed by one or two," Timofe said as he winked at Sergei and nodded toward Eugenia.

They laughed. Kostik did not. The three young men walked out of the house, down the porch stairs and as they approached the street, Ivan came to them. After they greeted each other, all four headed to Timoshenko's Bar.

CHAPTER TEN

Timoshenko's Bar was owned by Vasili Timoshenko who came from the Ukraine in 1898. He worked for several years in the Singer Sewing Machine factory, saved his money and with a few friends, built the bar. The bar soon became a successful business and frequented primarily by Ukrainian, Russian and Polish customers. The barroom itself, lit by gas, was clean with tables and chairs, a dance floor, and a small stage. Timoshenko was a fairly good-sized man for a Ukrainian and he kept a tight grip on the goings-on in the bar. Rarely did he have to throw someone out – which he did bodily when it became necessary. For the most part, Timoshenko's Bar was what in later years would be called a neighborhood bar, one that was there to serve a specific section of a community where everybody knew everybody. That is not to say it wouldn't get rowdy now and then. Generally, however, it was a safe haven after a week of hard work, hard twelve-hour-day work. Into this atmosphere Kostik was introduced to weekend fun.

"Have you ever had a drink, Kostik?" Timofe asked. "Anything at all? Beer? Vodka?"

"No," Kostik answered.

"Well, then, are you ready to break into a true and important part of life? You can't miss this. It's time you start," Sergei suggested. "Well?"

"I suppose so," answered Kostik not too enthusiastically.

By this time, a group of young women had joined the small group of people who had gathered to listen and watch this good-looking young man take his first drink. After they heard Timofe and Sergei say his name, they started to clap in unison and shout, "Drink, Kostik, drink. Drink, Kostik, drink." Ivan stood quietly off to the side of the group. He really did not like what was happening.

Kostik was beginning to feel embarrassed. Several of the men pulled the women toward Kostik and formed a circle around him. With that, the accordion player started playing a polka. One of the women broke from the circle and took Kostik by the hands and tried to get him to dance.

"I don't know how to dance," yelled Kostik.

"I will have to teach you," the young woman said in Russian. "My name is Stefania, Kostik.

Oh, look, they're bringing you some vodka. I will have a drink with you. Then we will dance."

Stefania was a very pretty woman, and she was not much older than Kostik; however, it was quite apparent that this was not her first time in Timoshenko's Bar nor her first time in these circumstances. Kostik was very naive and his ignorance regarding the goings-on was apparent. Stefania handed him a glass of vodka which Kostik drank down quickly, hoping to show how strong he was. He sputtered, coughed and started choking from the effect of the alcohol.

"Here, Kostik," Stefania said as she handed him another glass of vodka. "Drink this one slower. Let the vodka smooth the burn and you will be fine."

But Kostik wasn't fine. His empty stomach did not like being attacked by the liquor; neither did his brain, Stefania took advantage of what she saw. She pulled Kostik onto the dance floor and began turning him around in circles, catching him as he began to fall. After the fourth near-fall, Stefania let him drop to the floor. The crowd cheered as he tried to get up. He crawled his way to a wall and worked himself up on one of the chairs that was against the wall. Stefania then took Kostik by the arm and walked him out a side door.

Kostik did not have much money. As Stefania reached into one of his pockets to get what he did have, Ivan came up behind her, grabbed her arm, twisted it, slapped her face, said some not nice words and told her to go home. Just as this happened, Kostik vomited on Stefania and fell down. She screamed and swore and Ivan laughed at her, showing no mercy for her misfortune. It was then she realized she had drawn the attention of the crowd which made her cry; she ran away, presumably to go home.

Ivan took hold of Kostik and began his exit with him. He spotted Timofe and Sergei and let out with a stream of invectives to both of them for allowing Kostik to make such a fool of himself. After he had slept off the effects of the vodka, Ivan would make certain Kostik got an earful.

CHAPTER ELEVEN

Ivan half carried, half dragged and guided Kostik home. Kostik lost what was left in his stomach once again and dry-heaved several times after that. This would be a night he would long remember

Fortunately, when they got to the house, Eugenia was already asleep. Ivan did not have to tell Kostik not to talk when they got inside; he was not in a very talkative mood anyway. He was becoming a bit steadier on his feet, but Ivan held him to make sure he did not trip, fall or walk into something. They walked quickly into the bedroom where Ivan removed Kostik's clothes and got him into the bed. Kostik fell asleep immediately. Ivan took his clothes and put them under his other soiled clothing, so Eugenia wouldn't see them until she washed them. Hopefully, he thought, they would be dry and not smell so bad by then.

Ivan left the bedroom, closed the door and went out on the porch to wait for Timofe and Sergei.

He did not have to wait long. As soon as they arrived, he started in on them.

"What the hell did you two think you were doing to Kostik? Did you think it was fun? Did you think it was funny?"

"Oh, Ivan. It wasn't so bad," said Timofe.

"Wasn't so bad? He is just a kid. He told you he never drank in Russia. He trusted being out with you, and you knew that whore. How far were you going to let her do her thing? She took him outside and was trying to get the money she thought he had. I pulled her hand out of his pants pocket before she got what he had left of the dollar he made this week. Were you going to make up to him what she might have taken? No, of course not. You two should be ashamed of yourselves."

"What are you, his guardian?" Sergei asked angrily.

"I'll show you what guardian I am, my friend," Ivan said as he moved toward Sergei.

Timofe stepped between the two men.

"I'm sorry, Ivan. We should not have allowed it to happen, but let's not fight about it. That won't do anything to solve anything. You're right, it shouldn't have happened."

"I guess so," answered Sergei.

"Okay, it's time to go to sleep," said Ivan.

"Kostik is in the bed very asleep. I think you should sleep out here on the porch or on the floor in the bedroom. I'm not so sure that you will be in the bed with him in case he.....," Ivan gestured in the throw-up pose.

"You're right, Ivan," Timofe said smiling.

"All right, I'm going home. He's not going to be too happy in the morning. I don't know what Eugenia is going to say. She'll be disappointed with him – and with you two, too. I doubt if he is going to go to church. I'll come around before church to see how he's doing. Good night," said Ivan.

CHAPTER TWELVE

Kostik awoke Sunday morning – but, then again, he didn't. He raised his head but of its own volition, it fell back on the pillow which cradled it in the pocket which was made by his head not having moved for several hours. Fortunately, his stomach was quiet.

He tried to rise again and half succeeded – he fell sideways and almost went over the edge of the bed. As he caught himself, he let out a moan which wakened Sergei who was sleeping on the floor. He wasn't exactly in the greatest shape. Vodka doesn't let loose easily.

"How do you feel, Kostik?" Sergei asked softly.

"How does it look like I feel, Sergei? What happened last night? I feel lousy, my head hurts something terrible, my eyes don't like sunlight. I must have done some stupid things, but I don't know what."

"Kostik, you won't be the first and you won't be the last."

"Oh, that's just wonderful, Sergei. I've got to get up. My gosh – I don't have any clothes on."

"No you don't," said Ivan as he stepped into the room. "You were pretty messed up, Kostik.

Where are your clean clothes?"

Ivan got Kostik clean clothes, threw them to the bed and left the room. Sergei now in the bed, rolled over with his back to Kostik and was snoring seconds later. Kostik rose, put his pants on and went to the bathroom. He did not like what he saw in the mirror. He poured water into a bowl and splashed some of it on his face, dipped a cloth in the bowl, wrung it out and laid it across the back of his neck. The coolness felt good. He did it again and again. Finally, he dried himself off, put on the rest of his clothes and went into the kitchen. Eugenia eyed him with a cold stare.

"I know, I know, Eugenia," said Kostik. "You don't have to tell me."

"Oh, no? I don't have to tell you? Who said I don't.... you? What do you know? I told you to be careful. Were you? And, where are Sergei and Timofe? Wait until I get my hands on them!"

"I think they are still asleep," interjected Ivan. They were not too good when they came in."

"It's a good thing I didn't see them then," exclaimed Eugenia in a menacing tone. "They would not have entered this house – or the porch. They would have had to sleep on the grass. I'm only glad you were there, Ivan."

"Oh, I made certain I would be around, Eugenia. I just knew no good was going to happen the first night Kostik got paid. I hope he learned something from this."

"You are a good man, Ivan, and a friend I hope you appreciate, Kostik. He's like a big brother to you. I hope you know it."

"I know, and I thank you, Ivan," Kostik said quietly and humbly.

As is typical of a time like this in Eastern Europe, the two men hugged each other. They then sat down to drink tea and have breakfast. Kostik, however, really didn't feel like eating, but Ivan ate heartily. It wasn't long before Sergei and Timofe came into the kitchen.

"Look out, boys, Eugenia may get the broomstick after you," said Ivan smiling.

"We know. We know very much. Sergei and I talked. We are very sorry for what happened last night." Timofe spoke with difficulty, his voice showing the embarrassment he truly felt.

"It's over," interjected Kostik. "I will not let it happen to me again, and I don't want this to be talked about anymore," Kostik said with a very cold tone to his voice.

Kostik's tone hit Timofe and Sergei hard. Both young men apologized again to Kostik, but he would have none of it.

"You already said that. I'm sorry, too, that you let me make a fool of myself.

I don't want this to be talked about anymore, and here I am doing what I don't want. Do we all understand what I'm saying? I grew up last night. For that, I'm glad. Enough, all right?" Kostik stood up and walked into the bedroom where he threw himself on the bed. He was very angry – a little bit with Sergei and Timofe but very, very much with himself. "I'm so glad this happened here and not where my mother could have seen me," Kostik said under his breath to himself. "That would have been very bad. Thank you,

God, for Ivan being there. There is no telling where I would be this morning without him."

Kostik fell asleep and remained undisturbed well into the afternoon. When he awoke, he went into the kitchen where Eugenia was sitting, drinking tea.

"How do you feel now, Kostik? You slept a long time," Eugenia asked with a not-too-friendly bite to her voice.

"I will be fine, Eugenia. I said I grew up last night, and I mean what I say. I have some things I want to do; I will have to set my mind and get to them," Kostik said as he slapped his hand down on the table.

"Do you want some tea, Kostik?" asked Eugenia in a much softer tone. She was getting a message from Kostik that she thought she had heard earlier from him and was inwardly happy to hear that determination in his voice again.

"Yes, thank you. Tea would be very good right now," answered Kostik with a smile.

CHAPTER THIRTEEN

"What is it you want to do, Kostik?" asked Eugenia.

"First, I think I need to learn American. I will never lose my Russian language but I'm not in Russia now. I'm in America and America has its own language, and I want to become an American. I'm not throwing Russia away. I am bringing American alongside Russian. I will always be a Russian, but I want to be able to say I am an American. I will always have a place in my heart for Russia, but America is the country I have run away to. America is now my country and one way I can begin to be a part of it is to learn its language."

Eugenia began clapping and her eyes began tearing. Kostik heard another heavier clapping behind him. Unheard, Ivan had entered without a sound and listened quietly.

"Kostik, what you just said was wonderful. I feel embarrassed that I have done nothing like you are suggesting. Good luck. Maybe when you have learned American, you can help me. Those two out there should have heard you."

"Ivan, you can do it yourself," said Eugenia. "How long have you been in America?"

"Almost four years," replied Ivan.

"You're almost there. You have to be here five years, but you don't know any American, do you? How much can you talk in American?" asked Eugenia.

"Very little," said Ivan.

"So why did you come to the United States?" asked Kostik in a somewhat strong tone of voice.

"To get away from the Czar," Ivan stated emphatically. "He did no good for us little people."

"Well, why did you cross the ocean? Why didn't you go to Germany, France, Norway or Italy," retorted Kostik.

"Because I was told America had big opportunities, big chances for little people to become big people."

"Do you see opportunities?"

"I see little people still being little people."

"That's all you see?"

"Yes, dilapidated houses, men working long hours for little money and..."

"And what do the men do with their money," Kostik interrupted Ivan. "What do you see there, Ivan?"

"I don't know what you mean, Kostik."

"I know what I saw Saturday night, and I did not like it. I saw men who could hardly stand up.

I saw women - young and older - who were up to no good. What opportunities were they going after? Oh yes, they had the opportunity to do what they wanted to do, but is this why they came to America? Tell me, Ivan, did you believe America's streets were lined with gold like they told us over there, that everybody was rich, that everybody had big houses? Did you believe all that?"

"Did you, Kostik?" asked Ivan reflectively.

"You didn't answer me, Ivan."

"No, not all of it, Kostik, but I wanted to. Anything would have been better than what we had. You have to admit that, and what was said about America was something you wanted to dream about. You knew it was a story, but some of it had to be true.

Eugenia sat entranced, listening to these two. She sat between them, looking first left, then right, as she would have, had she been watching a tennis match.

"Kostik," she asked, but really meant telling him, "How did you get so smart so young?"

"I wonder if American is a hard language to learn. You've been here four years, Ivan. Why haven't you learned American?" Kostik furrowed his brow as he addressed Ivan.

"I don't know. I guess I am living where there are many Russians and I don't need to know American. Oh, maybe a little bit, but for the most part, I'm happy like it is."

"Where you work, everybody speaks Russian?" asked Kostik.

"Yes, it's a Russian company, owned by a Russian, and he hires only Russians," said Ivan somewhat testily.

"Does he speak American?" Eugenia entered the dialogue.

"Yes, Ivan, does he speak American? Everything he buys for his company he gets from Russia or other Russian-owned companies here in America?" Kostik spoke demonstrably with some derision.

"I don't know, Kostik," Ivan countered with some anger.

"I tell you answer – answer is no," spat Eugenia.

"I would say same thing," said Kostik. "Do you think your company will stay Russian? I say not. Some time he is going to have to hire Americans who can speak Russian, Americans who might know your job as good or better than you, and they can talk to other Americans which you can't. There comes a better job – like a foreman who has to talk to Russians and Americans. You have years on the job but can't talk to all the workers. What then, Ivan? Who gets the better job, do you think?"

Ivan didn't answer right away. He looked at Kostik. He looked at Eugenia. He looked down at the table. He looked into his cup of tea. Finally, he said, "Like Eugenia said, Kostik, how did you get so smart so young?" Eugenia and Ivan laughed. Kostik looked down and smiled.

"I talked so big about this that I better do something about it," Kostik offered quietly. "Do either of you know where the nearest school is where I could talk to a teacher. I better take an American who speaks Russian with me to tell what I want."

"I can take you to a school, but of course, I can't speak American," said Ivan. "Ask Sergei to go with you."

"Yes. Good. I'll ask him on Monday to go with me. You know, I have not written to my mother since I have been here. I should – no, I must do that now. Eugenia, do you have some paper and a pencil?"

"I have both," answered Eugenia. "You mean you have not written to her since you arrived? She has got to be worried sick. I'll get the paper and pencil and you sit down now and do it." Kostik spent the rest of the day writing his letter.

CHAPTER FOURTEEN

Monday seemed to drag because Kostik was anxious to find his American teacher. He had already spoken with Sergei who agreed to help him. Unfortunately, working from seven in the morning to seven at night, there really was no chance of finding a school open.

After work Monday, Kostik approached Sergei again.

"Sergei, if I go with you to him, would you talk with Smitty?"

"What do you want me to say?" asked Sergei.

Kostik told Sergei what to say. Sergei laughed which shocked and hurt Kostik.

"Do you really believe Smitty cares? Do you believe the company cares? Don't be silly! Just do your job and don't ask for trouble." Sergei spoke harshly, turned and walked away.

Kostik walked slowly toward Eugenia's house, kicking stones and pebbles lying in his path. At the house, Ivan was with Eugenia. Kostik told them what happened with Sergei.

"How am I to find a teacher? I know no one else who speaks Russian and American. I have to beg Sergei to do what I want him to do. Maybe if I had more money, maybe I could pay Sergei. But I don't have more money. Maybe Sergei is afraid to speak to Smitty, but Smitty won't hit Sergei, he won't hit me. What is so wrong with telling Smitty that I want to become an American? Who could be angry about that? What's so wrong with that?"

"It may be not so wrong as it might be a little jealousy that someone so young is trying to do something the other person has failed to do. Maybe he had chances to do what you want to do but didn't take advantage of them

Kostik, try him again. Ask him if he wants to be paid! If he says he does, ask how much. I may be able to give you some money," offered Ivan.

"I could maybe, too," said Eugenia.

Kostik looked at the two.

"You haven't got a lot of money, both of you," he said, his eyes welling up.

"We know you will pay us back," said Ivan. He looked down at the floor, tilted his face up and winked at Eugenia, "and since you're not going to the bar or dancing with those girls anymore, you will have money to pay us back."

They both then looked at Kostik with big smiles as Kostik looked back, started to laugh, shook his head and blurted out, "You smart alecks." The importance of what they had just said hit him. He moved to and hugged each. Here were two people who trust me and are trying to allow me to reach my dream, he thought to himself.

The next day Kostik approached Sergei again and asked him if he would talk to Smitty to which he answered, no, he would not. Kostik then asked him if he would if he paid him.

Sergei looked down at the floor, kicked at the floor in a shuffle move. He looked at Kostik as if he thought Kostik was crazy and said, "You're really serious about this. All right, yes, pay me to do this."

"How much do you want?"

"You don't have any money to pay me."

"How much?" Kostik asked angrily, angered that his friend would ask for pay when two other friends would support him in his try to better himself.

"Five dollars."

Ivan and Eugenia became very angry with Sergei when Kostik told them what Sergei said. They stood by their word. Each gave him two dollars and fifty cents.

Ivan said, "Kostik, tell Sergei you think five dollars is too much to just tell Smitty what you want to do. Tell him you'll give him three dollars. If he says no, then give him the five, but make sure you keep two dollars in a different pocket."

Kostik did what Ivan told him. Sergei laughed and said, "I don't want your money, Kostik. I thought about it and told myself that I should help you. Some day you might be able to do something for me."

"I thought you were a better friend than that and you proved that you are. Thank you, Sergei. Thank you very much."

They shook hands.

"Where did you get the money to pay me, Kostik? You don't have to tell me – I know, Ivan and Miss Nevar." Kostik nodded. "They are good friends, Kostik. You're lucky," Sergei said in a saddened voice.

Kostik picked up on the way Sergei said it but did not pursue it. He had thought about Sergei's loneliness during several other conversations they had had, but now was not the time to get into it Kostik thought.

CHAPTER FIFTEEN

At lunchtime, Sergei and Kostik went to sit with Smitty. Sergei nervously spoke, "Smitty, Kostik asked me to speak to you."

"Oh, yeah? About what?"

"He wants to become an American."

"What?" Smitty spouted out loudly.

"Yes, Smitty, and because I'm the only one he knows who speaks Russian and American, he needs....me....to....help....him." Sergei spoke haltingly.

"What's that got to do with me?" asked Smitty gruffly.

"Well, he wants to learn American language but by the time we get from work, schools are closed."

"They don't teach American to Russians or to Germans or Italians or to whoever," said Smitty.

"No, what he wants to do is hire a teacher who speaks Russian who can teach him American."

"Yeah, so like I said, what does that got to do with me?"

"Kostik wants to know if you could let me and him take time off to go to a school for me to talk to somebody about this."

"Are you nuts? Ask him if he's nuts. I ain't gonna let you guys off for this. Get back to work."

Sergei told Kostik what Smitty had said which Kostik said he had guessed by Smitty's voice and look on his face. Kostik stood and nodded to Smitty and walked back to where he was working.

The owner of the Tannery, Mr. Josef Kolkova, came into the factory the next day. He asked Smitty about how things were going. Smitty told the owner what Sergei had spoken to him about.

"What did you tell him, Smitty?" the owner asked, interested.

"I asked Sergei if he was nuts. No, I said and told them to get back to work."

The owner laughed. An immigrant himself, he put his hand on Smitty's shoulder and said, "Yes, Smitty, I like you looking out for my company, but let me ask you how do these men work?"

"Oh, they are good workers, and the Russian kid don't goof off. He's always asking for things to do when he finishes the things I told him I wanted done."

"All right then...here you have an immigrant who looks like he would be somebody you want to keep and here's a young kid who looks like he wants to take America serious. I wouldn't be surprised from what you told me, he probably wants to become an American citizen. What do you think?"

"Yeah, I guess so," Smitty answered questioningly.

"Well, what would you think if I said it's all right with me if you let Sergei take the kid to talk to somebody?"

"You mean it?" Smitty asked with disbelief in his voice.

"Yes, I mean it. Tell me, Smitty, how many immigrants have you known, here or anywhere – for example, among your friends or sitting at a bar having a beer and hear somebody mention that a foreigner asked his boss for time off to do what the kid wants?"

"I don't know nobody, and I ain't heard nobody even bring it up."

"I haven't ever heard of it either. I think this kid is quite different. So, how about it? Do you think some of your other workers wouldn't like it?"

"Well, when you say what you said to me, I can handle the other guys – just repeating what you said, but how many others are gonna ask the same thing?"

"Let's deal with that when it comes up – if it ever does. When do you want to let them go?"

"Tomorrow? I'll tell them at quitting time."

"That will be good, Smitty; oh, and don't take any money from them."

The two men shook hands and Smitty turned to leave. He smiled and thought to himself: Don't that beat all. I never would've believed it. Sergei had been watching Smitty and the owner and thought nothing of it until he saw Smitty smile and shake his head.

"What's up, Smitty? Is the boss giving us more money the way you were smiling and shaking your head?"

"I'll tell you later Sergei. Now, get back to your job." Said Smitty in a softer tone.

At quitting time, Smitty told Sergei and Kostik what the owner had said. Sergei was very surprised; Kostik became teary-eyed and thanked Smitty.

"You're not any more surprised than I am, Sergei, but he was pretty serious about it, and he spoke highly about you, Kostik."

Sergei translated for Kostik who, again, wiped his eyes with the back first of one hand, then the other. As they parted for the night, Sergei told Kostik he would come by his house in the morning and take him to a school.

Ivan was at the house talking with Eugenia when Kostik arrived from work. He walked in grinning widely.

"You look like a cat that just caught a mouse, Kostik. What happened?" asked Ivan.

"You look very happy," Eugenia offered.

"I am very, very happy. What a wonderful country this is. I have been worrying about this a lot and today, God made it happen," Kostik spoke, his voice breaking slightly. "The company owner is allowing Sergei to take me to a school to find a teacher to teach me American."

"Oh, Kostik, that is wonderful. Tell us what happened."

Kostik told them what he could and what Smitty had said as they were about to leave the plant. All three were smiling and laughing about what did happen and what was to happen the next morning.

CHAPTER SIXTEEN

As he said he would, Sergei came to the house. Eugenia let him in and yelled to Kostik to hurry. Sergei was as excited about this venture as Kostik was. Was he not an important cog in this international wheel?

When they got to the school, Sergei asked for the principal's office as Smitty had told him to do. The principal greeted these two immigrants with indifference and noticed that one was just a boy.

Somewhat gruffly he asked what he could do for them. Sergei tried his very best to speak strongly, but he was speaking to someone who represented authority and he became apprehensive. But as he got deeper into the explanation, he felt his nervousness dissipate and his hands become calm. He related the whole story, even going back to when Kostik brought up the subject in the plant and had been greeted with some ridicule. While Sergei talked, the Principal fidgeted somewhat discourteously with papers on the counter until he began to listen intently. This was an unusual tale. He stopped Sergei and invited both into his office, motioned for them to sit down and told Sergei to continue. When Sergei indicated he was finished, the Principal smiled and told them how impressed he was. He asked – after Sergei translated – how much of Kostik's background Sergei could tell him. He began asking questions. Where in Russia was Kostik from? How old is he? Where are his parents? When the principal was told Kostik came alone he shook his head slowly and raised his eyebrows. After asking a myriad of questions, he asked, "What can I help you – help Kostik – with?"

"Can you tell us where we can find a teacher who speaks Russian who could teach Kostik American?"

"I know of several. I have a young lady on my staff who could do it, but I'd have to ask her if she would be willing to."

"I understand," said Sergei and turned to tell Kostik what had been said. Kostik nodded. "When can I know?" he asked.

The principal chuckled, thinking to himself, this kid is nervous.

"I will ask the teacher at the end of our school day. How can I get in contact with you?"

"We could come back after work," offered Sergei. "What time do you stay here until?"

"I'm afraid you work longer hours than do we. We leave about five. By the way, from what you have told me, the owner of the company did not limit your time in getting this done; therefore, this period is almost finished. I will ask one of the office staff to take the teacher's class and have her come in here for a short introduction. Would that be all right with you?"

Sergei translated and Kostik was elated. The principal did not have to wait for a translation. He set things in motion and ten minutes later, the teacher entered the office.

"Sergei, Kostik, this is Miss Anna Polikov." The two stood and bowed, Kostik still adhered to the Russian traditions, Sergei had not lived long enough in America to have forgotten them or to have lost them on purpose.

"Miss Polikov was born in America to Russian parents and speaks both American and Russian fluently. Now, before we get started, will you, Sergei and Kostik, please let me speak with Miss Polikov alone. You may have a seat out in the waiting room where you came in."

The two jumped to their feet, bowed to Miss Polikov and the principal, turned and went out. Their actions brought a smile from Miss Polikov and approval from the principal as he closed his office door. The Principal and Miss Polikov talked for only twenty minutes. When the two came from the office, Kostik and Sergei jumped to their feet which brought another smile to Miss Polikov.

"Sergei," said the Principal, "tell Kostik that Miss Polikov feels honored to be asked to do this, and she is ready to start as soon as Kostik feels ready."

Sergei spoke to Kostik who threw back his head and yelled, "God be praised," at once showing embarrassment. Miss Polikov immediately crossed to Kostik to tell him what he had done was all right. She touched his shoulder at which Kostik grasped her hand and kissed it. Miss Polikov showed how much she appreciated that and told Kostik she recognized and understood the Russian gesture. She told him how much it pleased her that he had done it and now, was he ready to begin.

"May I take Kostik and Sergei to my classroom?" Anna asked the principal.

"Yes, of course. We have some time before we lock up the school," he answered. "You'll need to set up a schedule, a meeting place and how much you are going to charge Kostik."

"Can you help me with that?" she asked the principal. "I have no idea what to charge."

"Well, yes, we must remember his pay from the company." The principal asked Kostik through Sergei what his pay was and was taken aback when Kostik said one dollar a week. "I was not aware the pay was so low."

Sergei said he could not believe what Kostik said and told him so. Kostik repeated it.

"I'm getting along fine, Sergei, but ask her how much."

Sergei asked. "I don't know," she replied. "Certainly, he can't pay much." She turned to the principal who said Kostik cannot afford much but thought ten cents a week would be reasonable.

Miss Polikov agreed and said, "It's settled, but we had better ask Kostik if that's all right."

Kostik said that it was more than all right when he was asked and then asked when they could start; the first day was the very next day. They decided to get together twice a week after supper on the chosen days and it was up to Anna to tell Kostik when she had another free evening if Kostik were willing, which he certainly was.

CHAPTER SEVENTEEN

Sergei and Kostik entered the plant together the next day. Smitty saw them enter and quickly walked to meet them, giving away the excitement he felt for Kostik which he really did not want to show.

"So, what happened, Sergei?" asked Smitty, trying to keep his strong feeling from showing.

Sergei started to tell him everything from the beginning. It wasn't long before the other men joined the three of them; Smitty did not object. When it became apparent that Sergei had told the whole story, Smitty returned to his supervisory role.

"Okay, you guys, enough time lost. Work ain't getting done, so move it!" Strong words, but the tone of his voice was softer than the words.

Kostik felt a difference in the way his co-workers seemed to treat him. In the past, the other men rarely approached or even noticed him, but today the men nodded at him and smiled his way as they had not done before. It was a feeling of new-found respect that Kostik seemed to perceive. Although communication was virtually non-existent, Kostik was welcomed into a small group at lunch for the first time. He wondered how long it would last.

Kostik's meetings with Anna got off to a strong start which continued week after week. His progress was amazing. His American vocabulary expanded much more than Anna had expected, but his American grammar was a stumbling block. As much as Anna tried to get him to think in American, Kostik continued to place verbs and other parts of speech where they would be placed in a Russian sentence. Occasionally, in frustration, she would raise her voice which Kostik did not take well. He considered himself a disappointment to Anna when that happened and, therefore, a failure at that point. He apologized deeply which is not what Anna was looking for, and

59

she tried to get him to understand that. Anna saw that he was working too hard on his studies and was not allowing mistakes to be made. As this one session ended, she began to develop a plan to show Kostik really how well he was doing, and she also wanted to see for herself just what he was able to do in any everyday conversation he might get involved. She was certainly aware that his vocabulary was not extensive enough to carry on a truly meaningful conversation, but he knew enough to stumble through one that did not require deep thought or argumentative discourse.

The following day after her school day was over, she went to the tannery to talk with Kostik's supervisor.

"Hello. My name is Anna Polikov, Kostik's teacher. May I speak with you for a few minutes?"

Smitty was somewhat taken aback. "Hello, I am Harold Smith. Everybody calls me Smitty. I'm pleased to meet you and thank you for what you're doin' for Kostik. What can I do for you?"

"I would like to know when you and your men go to lunch. If they all stay here, would you allow me to join you during the lunch period? I want to see just how Kostik gets along joining a conversation with what he knows at this time, and if you would mind, tell me what you think of how he's doing. I know this must sound like a very strange request, but it will give me an idea of what I have to stress in my teaching, so he will know what to spend more time on studying and practicing."

"Holy cow, what a teacher!" Smitty blurted.

"No, not really," stated Anna. "This is a learning opportunity for me, too. I've never done anything like this, and I am very pleased that my principal has given me this opportunity. If you can arrange what I've asked of you, I – and I'm sure Kostik – will be very grateful."

"When would you want to do this?" asked Smitty, smiling inwardly, thinking with satisfaction that he again was going to be a part of Kostik's Americanization. "I, also, ain't never done nothing like this, but I feel very good being a part of the whole thing."

"You're a good boss, Mr. Smitty. This is what I want you to do. Ask Kostik to tell the story of how he got the idea to leave Russia and tell how difficult it was to do. Then, I will talk with Kostik later – after you have convinced him to do what you ask. Thank you, Mr. Smitty."

Smitty chuckled at Anna calling him "Mister" Smitty, but he certainly did not resent it; in fact, he liked hearing it. Smiling, he called to Kostik and Sergei.

"Kostik, I got an idea. I think you have been taking lessons a pretty long time. I think you might be ready to really start using what you have learned up. How 'bout it?"

Sergei translated. Kostik wanted to know what Smitty meant.

"I want Kostik to tell – in American – how he got the idea to come to America and how difficult the trip was."

"I don't know how to do that, Sergei," Kostik said, shaking his head, answering in Russian.

"Tell me what you just said in American," Sergei challenged Kostik.

Kostik looked at Sergei, not believing what he had just heard Sergei say. "I can't," Kostik answered in Russian.

"In American, Kostik, in American," Sergei said quietly in American. "Say, 'I can't' in American."

Kostik shook his head. "Nyet!" Kostik answered, again in Russian.

Sergei grabbed Kostik by the shoulders and shook him. "You didn't even try," Sergei said in Russian and, again, in American. "You see, I do it in both languages! How do you think I do that.... from TRYING!" Sergei yelled. "You not even going to try?" Sergei yelled in American.

Kostik turned and walked quickly away, scowling at Sergei. Smitty, standing nearby, having heard the loud voices, waved Sergei off just as Sergei began to go after Kostik.

"He won't even try to talk American, Smitty. What's he taking lessons for?"

"He'll be back, Sergei. He will realize how wrong he is, but it will take a little time. He first has to realize he's embarrassed, and he's got to figure out how to get around his embarrassment in front of his friend." Sergei shook his head and went back to work.

CHAPTER EIGHTEEN

Kostik left the plant at the end of the shift and walked angrily to Eugenia's house. Eugenia could see Kostik was angry and decided because he really looked very perturbed, not to ask him why. He would tell her in good time.

Kostik went to his room, closed the door and lay down on the bed. He closed his eyes, put his arms behind his head and shook his head slowly. Who am I most mad at, me or Sergei? Am I mad at me because I'm afraid? Afraid of what? Afraid to make a mistake? Afraid to embarrass me? Afraid? That's not good. I've got to show what I've learned sometime. Sergei is a good friend. I wouldn't be lying here concerned about what was asked of me if it weren't for Sergei getting involved. Kostik rolled over and closed his eyes again. Within a few minutes, he sat up suddenly and said to himself what a jerk he was – and is. He rolled out of bed, stood up and walked to the kitchen.

"Feeling better, Kostik?" Eugenia asked. "Have you calmed down?"

"You could tell I was angry?" Kostik asked.

"You couldn't tell different, Kostik?" Eugenia said looking down at the table for a short while. When she looked up, she asked, "Are you going to tell me?"

Kostik told her everything.

"What's the matter with you, Kostik? What is wrong with what they wanted you to do? Nothing! Okay, I think from now on I'm not going to talk Russian to you. I am only going to talk American to you. What do you think about that, Kostik?" Eugenia stated in rather a strong tone.

Kostik smiled. "I think that's probably a good idea, Eugenia."

"You know that's a good idea, and I think you better go tell Anna what happened today."

"I will. I will tell her."

At his next session with Anna, Kostik told her what happened. "How do you feel about that Kostik?" she asked.

"I am sorry at what happened, but I think I know why I felt so strongly," Kostik said.

"Why, Kostik?"

"Because I don't speak good American. Listen to you. You don't have any, how you say, accent. My accent is big," spoke Kostik quietly.

"Kostik, what you're telling me is your hesitancy – you know what I mean when I say 'hesitancy'?"

"Not exactly," replied Kostik.

Anna explained what the word meant and then added, "There is nothing wrong with having an accent. It is showing that you are trying to learn the language of your new country. It shows that you want to become a part of this new country's people. If you have the accent until you die, you will have shown how strongly you felt about becoming an American. You should not be ashamed of your accent; you should be proud of what you are doing."

"Do you really mean that? I mean, is that what you think?" asked Kostik. "Do you believe that people will truly think the way you say?"

"There will always be those who look down on anyone who talks differently. They have more of a problem than you do, but most people will understand. Remember, Kostik, everyone here – and I mean everyone! – is going to be speaking differently. The question is, differently from what? Who is to say whose accent is correct? Are you – or is anyone – going to say your accent is better – or worse than my father's accent? The important thing is whether your American is clear – more understandable than the American my father speaks. Are you understandable when you speak American? I will tell you that right now you are understandable, much better than when you first started speaking, and you will become more so the longer you speak it. As I said, Kostik, you may never lose your accent, but it will become less of a problem over time." Anna studied Kostik as she spoke and was satisfied that her words were getting through. She was pleased that the hurdle had been overcome, she thought, at least at the present. It appeared that Kostik had absorbed every word she had driven home, which he had.

"One more thing, Kostik. You had told me you wanted to go to Linden to find your friend, Andy Gorelick, from your village in Russia. I believe you can do it now. You know enough American to ask questions. Just take your time, talk slowly and as clearly as you can. Now, let's practice. Ask me the questions that you will ask the people in Linden," Anna said smiling at Kostik. What Anna said took Kostik completely off guard. He didn't know what to say, what to ask, how to ask it.

"Well, Kostik, talk to me," said Anna.

"I don't know how to say," answered Kostik.

"What are you trying to do?" asked Anna.

"You know what I want do," said Kostik, somewhat harshly.

"Can you start it in Russian? I don't like this, but this is something very new to you. So if you knew the person you were asking would understand you in Russian, what would you say?"

Kostik started the question in Russian.

"Good, Kostik. Now tell me what you just said in American," Anna interrupted.

"I want to find a man called Andy Garelick. I know he lives in Linden. Do you know him? Do you know where he lives? Can you tell me how to go to his house? Thank you."

Kostik looked at her, smiled and translated. For over an hour, Kostik slowly asked his questions – over and over again. Finally, he walked to Anna, hugged her and thanked her.

"I think I'm ready, Anna" Kostik said.

"I know you are," Anna answered. "Now, go to Linden."

CHAPTER NINETEEN

Kostik mulled it over in his mind – what do I say to Andy? What do we talk about? Why am I worried about this meeting? Anyhow, I will go to see him – soon. In the meantime, he had a job to go to.

"Hey, Kostik, come here," Smitty called across the room. Smitty then told Kostik he wanted the buildup of trash in the back area of the factory cleaned up. Suddenly, Kostik let out a loud yell as he fell to the floor. He had stepped on a board with a nail protruding from it that was now stuck deeply in his foot. Smitty and a few of the men ran to Kostik. Smitty kneeled by Kostik and said, "Hold on, Kostik. I'm gonna pull this out. I'll do it slow first to see if it will come. Sergei, hold his leg so it don't move when I pull."

Kostik was in pain, his eyes tearing. "That is all right, Smitty. Do what you have to do," he said.

Smitty gripped the board in such a way to make sure he could pull the nail straight out. He pulled, but the nail was stuck.

"Kostik, I am gonna have to turn it to make it move. I'll do it easy."

Kostik screamed as Smitty twisted the board and Kostik tried to move his leg. Fortunately, Sergei held the leg tight, preventing it from moving. Smitty pulled. The nail came out. Kostik's foot did not bleed much but the nail was covered with rust.

"We better wash his foot," said Smitty. "Sergei, run get me soap, hot water and a towel. Kostik, I think we gotta get you to a doctor."

Sergei came to clean the wound. The hot water hurt, but it was difficult to see if any dirt was being removed from the wound. Once washed, Sergei and Smitty wrapped the towel around Kostik's foot, got him up and ready to go to St. Elizabeth Hospital in Elizabeth.

Fortunately, the trolley was not far for several men to help carry Kostik to the trolley. The men put Kostik on the car and two of the men stayed with him. When they arrived at the hospital, they helped him off the trolley and into the hospital where a doctor and two nurses began caring for him.

The nurses applied a wet towel with warm water and soap. Having cleaned the wound, the doctor began to examine the damage.

"Get me a bottle of iodine," the doctor instructed one of the nurses. "This is going to hurt, young man. Of course, not as bad as that nail, but you will feel the iodine for a while."

Following the treatment, the doctor and nurses bandaged the wound. "We have done all we can right now. It's up to your body to fight any infection, but you are going to have to keep the area around your wound as clean as possible. I would suggest you come back in a few days so we can make certain infection has not set in." The doctor tried to be as affirmative as possible.

"Thank you, doctor," Kostik said and bowed. "I will try to come back in three or four days." As he was leaving, they gave him a pair of crutches and the time to pay for them.

When they returned to the tannery, Kostik explained what the doctor had said, especially about keeping the wound clean.

"I don't know how we're gonna do that here," said Smitty. "Are you gonna be able to work, Kostik?"

"I have to, Smitty," answered Kostik. "I will think of something."

When Eugenia saw Kostik, she immediately cried. He started to explain what had happened when Ivan walked in. As he explained, Eugenia would not stop sobbing.

"Eugenia," Kostik said quietly, "Would you please make us some tea? I think we could all use it." Ivan smiled so Eugenia could not see him.

"Yes, yes. I will make us some tea. Just a moment, and I will get to it," Eugenia spoke uneasily.

"How much did the hospital charge you?" asked Ivan.

"Three dollars for the treatments and seventy-five cents for the crutches," said Kostik.

"You don't have that much money, Kostik," Eugenia called over her shoulder.

"I will have to save it," said Kostik as he lowered his head, knowing how difficult it will be on his wages.

Ivan looking directly at Eugenia said, "We will help you pay, Kostik. We know you will pay us, so no say no." Eugenia was nodding her head in agreement.

Kostik just shook his head and said thank you.

Kostik was able to move fairly well with his crutches and went back to the factory after two days of staying off his feet.

"Does your foot hurt bad?" asked Smitty when Kostik entered the factory.

"Not bad," answered Kostik. "I have to walk easy on that foot, that's all to it."

"You're not going to lose pay, Kostik, the boss said," Smitty told Kostik.

"What should I say, Smitty?" Kostik asked.

"Just tell him thank you when you see him. Now, what do you want to do? What can you do, do you think?"

"I can go to the back and do what I started to do, but this time, I will look out for nails," Kostik said with a laugh.

"I don't know, Kostik. Can you stand on that foot?" asked Smitty.

"I can stand easy. Anyway, I'll look out. When I'm tired, I'll sit, if that's all right."

"Yeah, that's all right. The other men understand and, Kostik, quite honestly, they think you're nuts."

Two weeks went by before Kostik went back to the hospital. When the bandage was removed, the nurses looked at the wound, looked at Kostik and left the room to get the doctor.

"Kostik, I don't like what this looks like," said the doctor. "I'm going to try to clean it again and then we'll talk."

The wound had begun to turn dark. This was not a good sign. The nurses did not hide their concern.

"Kostik, I don't like what I am seeing," said the doctor.

"What are you saying," asked Kostik.

"I am going to see if I can get another doctor to look at it. Dr. Stine has more experience with this kind of wound. Come back tomorrow about this time, and I will try to get Dr. Stine here to look."

The next day Kostik with the help of Eugenia, hobbled back to the hospital. It was not an easy journey for him, but he could not afford the trolley. He stubbornly refused to allow Eugenia to pay for it.

The nurses greeted Kostik and escorted him to a chair. A nurse went to find Dr. Stine.

"Hello, Kopituk. I am Dr. Stine. I'm told you stepped on a rusty nail, not a good thing to do." His attempt at humor fell very flat.

The nurses and Dr. Stine got Kostik up on a table and began to remove his bandages. When the last of the bandage was removed, Dr. Stine let out a whistle.

"This is not looking good," Dr. Stine said gruffly. He roughly inserted one of his instruments into the wound which caused Kostik to cry out and brought tears to his eyes. Dr. Stine looked harshly at Kostik and probed again, causing him to cry out in pain.

"This is the least of what you're going to feel, Kopituk. I'll be back in a few minutes," Dr. Stine said coldly and turned to leave the room.

One nurse whispered to the other, "I don't like Dr. Stine. He is not a nice man." Her whisper was loud enough for Kostik and Eugenia to hear. They agreed with her.

Dr. Stine returned with the doctor who first tended to Kostik.

"Well, Kopituk, that nail did some heavy initial damage to you; furthermore, it is continuing to do its nasty work. Your wound has become infected and the infection has begun to spread. It has spread enough to where there is only one way to stop it."

He stopped talking and looked around as if to make sure everyone was listening, everyone was waiting with great anticipation his next utterance, waiting to hear his learned conclusion which he deliberately failed to impart.

Much to Dr. Stine's dislike, Eugenia broke the silence. "What are you trying to say, Doctor?" she asked. "What is going to stop it, and stop it from what?"

"Stop it from going further, Madam. Stop the infection from spreading through his whole body, Madam," Dr. Stine answered haughtily. "If this happens, we will have no chance of stopping it. The only way now is to amputate his lower leg."

Everyone but Dr. Stine was stunned. Eugenia screamed. The nurses sucked in their breaths; one began to cry.

Kostik glared at Dr. Stine. "You are crazy, Doctor. That is all you can offer me? Make me a cripple?"

"No, Kopituk. I'm not crazy. I can also offer you something else – a grave."

"I will think about it," said Kostik.

"There is nothing to think about," answered Dr. Stine. "You don't have a lot of time." With that, he stomped out of the room and left the hospital.

One of the nurses spoke up. "I don't know him, but I have been told that there is a young doctor who recently graduated from medical school. His name is Dr. Martin Stein, and he has a good reputation. Maybe he has some newer ideas. I don't think he is related to this doctor because he spells his name differently."

Kostik tried to calm himself but his voice gave his anxiety and fear away. "Where is he, nurse? Do you know how I can find him?"

"No, I don't," she answered.

"Do you know, Doctor?" Kostik asked the other doctor.

"I believe his office is in Elmora," the doctor answered.

"What is Elmora? Where is Elmora?" asked Kostik impatiently.

"It's a part of Elizabeth near Roselle," said the doctor.

"Well, you heard what is going on, Doctor. Don't you have anything to say?" asked Kostik.

"It's true what he says about infection, but I'm not a surgeon, and I don't know how bad it is now."

"How do I go to Elmora," asked Kostik.

"You could walk there, Mr. Kopituk, but with your foot like it is, you better take the trolley," said the doctor. He told him where to catch the trolley to Elmora. "When you get to Elmora, you can ask where this Dr. Stein's office is located."

"How much costs trolley?" asked Kostik as he reached into his pockets to see how much money he had.

"To get to Elmora, it shouldn't cost more than five cents," said one of the nurses.

Kostik found enough change to get him to and from Elmora. He thanked everyone.

"I'm going with you, Kostik," said Eugenia.

"I was hoping you would go with me, Eugenia, but I didn't want to impose."

"Oh, for crying out loud, Kostik, you can get me so mad," Eugenia said rather strongly to Kostik.

The two of them left the hospital and walked to the nearest trolley stop. The trolley conductor said he would tell them when to get off and since he knew of Dr. Stein, he would tell them which way to walk to his office. Throughout this trip to Elmora, Kostik sat quietly, did not talk and looked out the window and down at his lap and folded hands. Occasionally, he shook as if a cold wind wafted over him. He was definitely very frightened. His eyes welled several times. He turned his head so Eugenia would not see. She saw, but said nothing. She knew he would be embarrassed if she said anything.

When they reached Elmora, the conductor signaled to Kostik and Eugenia to leave the trolley car. He told them which way to walk and told them Dr. Stein's office would be on the right, not far from where they now were.

They saw the sign that Dr. Stein had in front of his office before they got there.

"Are you all right, Kostik?"

"I think so, Eugenia. I hope he can tell me something better than that other doctor."

"I hope so, too." said Eugenia as she knocked on the door.

The door was opened by a slight man who welcomed them in. "I am Dr. Martin Stein, and I certainly hope I can help you. Come in and sit down. What are your names?" Kostik and Eugenia introduced themselves.

"So, you are not this young man's mother, Miss Nevar?"

"No, he is one of three young men who board with me," she answered. "Kostik is a hard worker, but he doesn't make much money, doctor. I and his friends will help pay you...." her voice trailed off.

"His wages are pretty low?"

"Yes."

"Let's me look at his injury," said Dr. Stein.

The doctor sat Kostik on a table and removed the bandage. "Yes, this does not look good. Who took care of this wound?" asked Dr. Stein.

"Dr. Stine at St. Elizabeth Hospital. He told me he would have to cut off my leg to save me," Kostik said, his voice quivering.

Dr. Stein said nothing. He pulled out a magnifying glass and looked very closely at the wound.

"It does not look good, but I don't see it requiring amputation. What I'm going to do will hurt you, young man. I'm sorry, but it has to be done," Dr. Stein said to Kostik.

"Do what you have to do, doctor. I will understand."

Dr. Stein washed the wound with hot water and a clean towel. He then dried it, causing Kostik to moan. Next, the doctor looked at Kostik, told him that the iodine was going to burn, asked if he was ready and as Kostik said yes, he poured the liquid into the wound. He dipped a corner of the towel into the wound. Satisfied with what he saw, Dr. Stein repeated the procedure. After a few minutes, he dried it again.

"We'll see if this treatment is effective. I want you to come back tomorrow. No, on second thought, I want you to stay here tonight. I will look at it again first thing in the morning." He then bandaged the foot again, but not as tightly as it had been.

"Is it all right for you to go back by yourself, Miss Nevar?" Dr. Stein asked.

"I will be all right, doctor," Eugenia answered.

CHAPTER TWENTY

Dr. Stein and Kostik spent a nice evening together. Dr. Stein was so enthralled with Kostik's story of his escape from Russia, he questioned him profusely. Early the next morning, Kostik was back on the table having his bandages removed.

"I don't see enough change – good or bad – to make a major decision, Kostik. I'm going to send you home and ask you to come back in three days; but, first I'm going to treat it again," Dr. Stein told Kostik. "I want to watch it closely. I don't see anything for you to worry about right now."

"Do you mean there could be something for me to worry about later?" asked Kostik.

"I cannot tell you no, but neither will I tell you yes. All I will say is we will watch it," said Dr. Stein.

As Kostik started out of the office to catch the trolley, Dr. Stein stopped him. "Wait just a moment, Kostik. I have to go to Elizabeth today, and I might as well go now; so, I will drive you to Miss Nevar's house."

Before he drove away from Eugenia's house, Dr. Stein warned Kostik, "I know you are going to go to work tomorrow. Kostik, your bandage must be kept clean. I cannot tell you strongly enough: it MUST be kept clean."

Eugenia had a bin of clean rags long enough to wrap around the foot over the bandage. She and Kostik practiced how to wrap the bandage securely.

"I will go to work with you, Kostik. We don't want any dirt to get on your foot, and you have to go back to the doctor in three days?"

"Yes," Kostik answered, "three days."

All of the men were glad to see Kostik back. Smitty reminded him to be careful and not to rush. Later in the morning, the company owner came in.

"Is Kopituk here, Smitty? I'd like to talk to him," the owner said.

"Yeah, he's in the back cleaning the area. I'll get him," Smitty said as he walked to the back.

Kostik came with Smitty. He tried to show he was better than he actually was, but his walking with crutches gave his pain and faltering away more than he liked.

"Mr. Kolkova, how are you, sir?" Kostik asked, extending his hand with some difficulty.

"No, no, Kostik. The question is how are you?" Mr. Kolkova returned the greeting. "Tell me what is happening with your injury and, truly, how are you getting along?"

Kostik recounted the entire ordeal.

"Just a moment, Kostik. Let us sit down. You don't look comfortable," Kolkova interrupted.

"Thank you, sir. I am not comfortable," offered Kostik.

Kostik did not hold back his unfavorable opinion of Dr. Stine. His tone of voice brought a smile to Kolkova for which he apologized.

"I'm not laughing, Kostik. I am smiling at your obvious dislike for Dr. Stine strongly conveyed in your tone of voice. I admire your discussion with him and your decision. You do know what will happen to you if that infection spreads. You do know that it can kill you," Kolkova spoke slowly. "You do understand that?" he questioned.

"Yes, sir. I know that, but I am not finished with what I have to tell you," said Kostik.

Kostik went on to tell Kolkova about Dr. Stein – the second one – and what he has been doing for Kostik. He did not tell him about the difficulty he has in getting to Dr. Stein's office.

"Well, I am surprised about this young doctor. I hope he is going to cure the infection in your leg. But I am going to tell you this, Kostik. I am going to pay the hospital, pay Dr. Stine off and pay Dr. Martin Stein his fees. I'm also increasing your wage to two dollars a week."

Kostik looked at Mr. Kolkova, then at Smitty, then back to Kolkova. Tears filled his eyes and rolled down his cheeks. He could not speak. He reached for Kolkova's hands, bowed his head to them and kissed them which took Kolkova completely aback.

"Now you don't have to do that, son," said Kolkova, his voice breaking.

"You know our traditions, Mr. Kolkova. How else can I thank you? I cannot believe what you are doing for me."

Both stood; Kolkova came to Kostik and hugged him. Smitty, somewhat at a loss with what he was seeing, backed quietly away from the two of them.

Kostik was the first to speak. "Thank you, Mr. Kolkova. I am going back to work. I am going to write my mother and tell her what you have done – everything."

With that, he turned to leave, but stopped, turned to Kolkova and with a big grin, said "Maybe I should go and step on another nail."

Kolkova laughed; Kostik waved a salute and left laughing.

Over the next several weeks, Kostik went to Dr. Stein who checked the progress of the wound. Healing was satisfactory enough that Dr. Stein told Kostik he was out of danger. However, he wanted to see Kostik in one week and then two weeks after that. Until then, keep the bandage on and clean.

"I know it's been a long ordeal for you, Kostik, but, it is almost over. You have been very fortunate," said Dr. Stein.

"What has made me, like you say, fortunate, has been my luck to find you, Doctor. You have saved me," said Kostik.

"Thank you Kostik, but you have done very well in protecting yourself. Hopefully, full recovery is only a short time coming."

The three weeks seemed endless for Kostik, but finally, his wound totally healed. His decision had been the correct one, as was his decision to keep Dr. Martin Stein as his permanent physician.

CHAPTER TWENTY-ONE

Kostik walked every day to make sure his foot still felt good and he would be able to walk to Linden where Andy Gorelick lived.

He asked Ivan what road he should take to get to Linden. He decided to go on Sunday, so on Saturday night, he went to sleep early and asked Eugenia to wake him in the morning.

Eugenia wakened Kostik and made him come into the kitchen. They had breakfast together and talked about how glad he would be see Gorelick again. Andy was a few years older than Kostik but being able to talk to and reminisce with someone from Pinsk excited him.

When they finished breakfast, Kostik hugged and thanked Eugenia, who unexpectedly gave him food to eat on the trip.

Three hours later, Kostik was in Linden. He approached several people and asked if they knew Gorelick. Over an hour passed before he found someone who knew him. Following the directions Kostik was given, he walked to the site of Andy's store which supported his business. It was a business about which Kostik knew nothing, but it was one which allowed Andy to use many of the things in his carpentry business: toilets, sinks, bathtubs, fencing and much more. Andy remodeled houses and was doing quite well.

Kostik walked into the yard where Andy had all of this "junk", which he called it, haphazardly spread around.

Andy came out of his small house. "You looking for something?" he said.

"Yes, I am looking for Andy Gorelick," answered Kostik.

"I am Gorelick. Who are you?"

"Andy, I am Kostik Kopituk from Pinsk," said Kostik. Gorelick looked very shocked. He stared at Kostik for a few seconds and said, "You mean it?"

"I mean it," answered Kostik. "I have been trying to come see you for a long time and finally had the chance today."

Gorelick did not know what to do or say. After a half-minute, he lunged forward and wrapped his arms around Kostik who reacted in kind. Both men began crying and talking at once. Both stopped talking. Both started talking. Both laughed.

"Come, Kostik. Come to the house. We have much to talk about."

So began several hours of "did you know...?", "do you remember...?", "have you heard from...?" Kostik said, "I had better start walking back, Andy."

"No, Kostik, I will drive you in my truck," said Andy. "But, it is starting to get late, and I don't like to drive at night."

"Let me ask you something, Andy. Is there some way you could teach me what you do?"

"Yeah, but it would be difficult for you. The best way for you to learn would be to work with me."

"How long would it take?" Kostik asked.

"I could teach you the fundamentals in about two months. If you run into problems, I could come and help you. But, I think you would know not to take jobs that are too big for you."

With that, they drove off to Elizabethport. They talked small talk until they reached Eugenia's house.

"Andy, I will think about what you said. Thank you very much."

"I have enjoyed our meeting today, Kostik. I will wait to hear from you. My offer to you will stay. Just let me know what you would like to do."

Eugenia was waiting for Kostik to tell her everything, and she was full of questions until Kostik said he had to go to sleep so he could go to work in the morning.

CHAPTER TWENTY-TWO

Kostik began to seriously think about what Gorelick had said to him. He realized that there wasn't much of a future for him at the tannery but after what Mr. Kolkova offered to do for him, he felt uneasy about quitting at this time.

Of course, he thought, "I don't even know what it is that I would be getting into, or if the future would have for me more than I could get from the tannery. I don't have carpentry tools. I don't know anybody who would hire me. I don't have a way to carry my tools to jobs. I don't have a way to get to any jobs I would get. What am I thinking? I can't buy a car. I can't even buy a truck! What are you thinking, Kostik?"

He was sitting on the porch of Eugenia's house. He started out toward the street, looked down at the floor, looked out toward the street and shook his head.

"What are you shaking your head for, Kostik?" shouted Ivan as he turned in from the sidewalk.

"Hello, Ivan. I am glad you are here. I have to talk to you."

"My goodness, what is so serious?" asked Ivan. "Let me sit down and you can tell me."

When Eugenia heard them talking, she came out.

"Hello, Ivan. Nice to see you."

"Hello, Eugenia. You are just in time, too. Kostik has something serious to talk about."

Kostik told them about what Gorelick told him and what he was thinking. He repeated to them virtually all the reasons for his not attempting to leave the tannery and going with Gorelick.

"Are you hearing what you are saying, Kostik?" asked Ivan.

"So what? I know what I am saying."

"What are you doing here, Kostik? How did you get here? Did you ask yourself in Russia what you are asking yourself here? What kind of answers did you give yourself over there? You must not have given yourself the same answers you seem to be giving yourself here."

Kostik had nothing to say.

"Well, Kostik?" said Ivan. "Talk to me. Tell me what you are thinking now."

"I feel ashamed, Ivan. That's why I need you, my friend. Didn't take you long to get me to think sensibly; but, Ivan, my questions still have to be answered. I just now have to think how best to answer them."

"That's right, young man. How about you, Eugenia? You haven't said anything – which I think is very unusual." All three laughed.

"Have you answered any of your questions, Kostik?" Eugenia asked.

"What do you mean, Eugenia? I can't answer them because I don't have any answers," he said rather huffily. "Where am I going to get tools? How do I carry those tools if I were to get them? I can't buy a car. I can't buy a truck. I can't..." Kostik is cut off by Ivan.

"All I hear, Kostik, is what you can't do. What can you do to get what you want, and what is it that you want? Yes, just exactly what is it that you want? Do you know? Do you have any idea?"

"Yes, I know. What I don't know is how to get there, and you are not helping me by repeating my questions to me."

"What is it that you want me to do?" asked Ivan.

"Yes, what is it you want Ivan to do, Kostik?" asked Eugenia.

"All I want is for you to give me some ideas," said Kostik, "both of you."

"All right, Kostik, here's an idea. Go back to Gorelick. No, wait – get a piece of paper and a pencil. Write down all the questions you are asking yourself. Then, go to see Gorelick again. Give him the list of questions. Ask him if he asked himself any questions like that. If he did, how did he answer them. Did he use his answers? How did he use them? Did he use the answers to get him started? What did it take for him to get started? There's my idea, Kostik. Can you use it? Will you use it?" Ivan looked straight at Kostik while he spoke.

"That is a good idea, Ivan. I will do it. Thank you," Kostik said quietly while his mind was racing. He went into the kitchen, found some paper and a pencil, sat down at the table and began writing his questions.

After finishing what he thought were all his questions, he sat back and began reading them to himself. They looked different on paper than they did in his mind. They didn't look so menacing he told himself. He also told himself that in time he could answer all those questions. It's time for me to go to Gorelick.

Kostik could not believe that five o'clock Saturday morning would ever come, for he had been tossing and turning for hours. Eugenia expected to have to wake Kostik, but he was almost fully dressed.

"Come for breakfast, Kostik," Eugenia called.

She had the meal ready: sliced orange, buttered bread with strawberry jam, eggs in the pan ready to be put on Kostik's plate.

"Eugenia, this breakfast is too good," exclaimed Kostik.

"Enjoy, Kostik. Then, you have to leave quickly."

He ate very fast, stood, hugged Eugenia and left the house. It would not take him as long this time because he knew now where Gorelick lived.

"Good morning, Kostik. What time did you leave Miss Nevar's house... one o'clock?" Andy asked laughing.

"Hello, Andy. No, I was excited to come today to talk to you. I have something I want you to see."

"What is all this, Kostik?" Andy asked as Kostik handed him the papers with all the questions.

Kostik explained what he had done – asking himself all these questions that he wanted Andy to comment on.

Andy sat quietly, just reading the questions to himself. He said nothing to Kostik. When he had read through all of the questions, he smiled at Kostik and said, "Kostik, did you ask yourself all these questions before you left Russia?"

"No, Andy, all my thinking was about how to escape. Was any of your thinking like any of my questions?"

"Yes, but you have to remember, I had been working in Russia for a lot more years than you had. I saved a lot of my money. For what, I didn't know when I started to save my rubles, but when I began to think America, then I knew – but only that I would take the money with me. It is what got me into the United States. I didn't have a name of a sponsor like you did – even though I didn't know you – or know even that you were coming," Andy said with a smile.

Andy saw that it appeared that that comment made Kostik uncomfortable.

"No, no, Kostik. I think that was very smart of you to use me," Andy said in a soft voice as he put his hand on Kostik's shoulder. "Now, let's talk about these questions."

CHAPTER TWENTY-THREE

For the next several hours, the men discussed each question. For every negative comment from Kostik, Andy was able to counter with a positive approach. He drew on his experience from his working days in Russia. Before too long, Andy began wearing Kostik down.

"Andy, let's go back to the beginning. I want to use what you have said to see if I can come up with more things that tell us I can be sure of everything working out."

"That's good, Kostik, but everything is not going to work the way you want it all the time. Don't build up what's not there because if it doesn't happen the way you want it, you can – especially since you are new at this – get discouraged. You don't want that."

"Yes, you're right, Andy," answered Kostik. "But, you know what I got to do now? I got to think about all we talked about, especially what you are telling me."

"Now wait a minute, Kostik. I am not a real smart man and what I've told you may not work for you. I am talking from my experience."

"I know that, Andy. What I have to do is put myself in those situations and see how I fit. If I don't fit, how can I use what you said and make it fit me."

"Let me know when you want to start with me. But, be very sure you want to do this, Kostik. You know, this can seem very exciting. Something new. Something that's going to be yours, all yours. Remember – it can fail also."

"Oh, that's a fine how do you do, Andy," said Kostik, not happy with that last admonition.

"Kostik..." Andy didn't finish what he was going to say.

"I'm sorry, Andy. You are right. I am getting stars in my eyes. You are right to bring me down to the ground," said Kostik.

"Okay, Kostik. You have to think about all we talked about today. It may keep you awake tonight. Don't rush. You have people who are getting to know you. You're building a good reputation, or the owner of the company would not be doing for you what he is doing. Just take your time. From what you have told me about what he has done for you, I think he already knows that you're not a lifelong employee. It would not surprise me if he helps you get your new job going."

"You're a real smart man, Andy. I'm very thankful for your advice and, yes, even grateful for it," said Kostik.

"Oh, shut up, Kostik. I haven't done nothing. Now, I think it's time for me to drive you home," said Andy with a smile of satisfaction on his face. It made Andy feel very good that this young man recognized him in such a way.

Eugenia and Ivan were sitting on the porch when Andy drove up. Kostik let himself out of the truck, shook hands with Andy, thanked him and closed the door.

"Well, what did you do all day, Kostik?" Ivan asked.

"I don't know where to start to tell you. I had a very good lesson from Andy Gorelick," Kostik answered.

"Lesson? What kind of lesson?" asked Eugenia.

Kostik started telling them what had happened and the more he explained, the more excited he became.

"Whoa, Kostik, slow down," said Ivan. "You really are excited about this new adventure, aren't you?"

"Yes, I am. My problem is how to get it all together in my mind. There is so much to think about. Where do I start?" Kostik spoke more to himself than to the two who sat listening with great interest.

Several weeks passed during which Kostik wrestled with his decision to eventually leave the tannery and branch out into another new life. When and how was he going to tell Mr. Kolkova? This was growing into a major mental block for Kostik. Maybe I should talk with Smitty. Does he think Mr. Kolkova is going to be mad? Is he going to yell at me and fire me? Well, there's only one way to find out!

CHAPTER TWENTY-FOUR

Kostik arrived at the plant early. He needed to speak to Sergei because what he could not explain in American to Smitty, he needed Sergei to translate.

"You want me to do what?" asked Sergei.

"You will hear my whole story when we meet with Smitty," replied Kostik. "But, I have something to ask you Sergei. When you spoke with Smitty and my name was said, what did Smitty say about me?" Kostik asked, looking straight at Sergei.

Kostik could not help noticing Sergei fidgeting. "So, he did talk to you about me," Kostik said. "Tell me, Sergei. It is important for me to know before I talk to him."

Sergei looked around to see whether anyone was within earshot. "Okay, Kostik, I'll tell you. You might like it, you might not."

"What? What? Tell me, Sergei."

"All right. Smitty said he didn't think you would be working here very long, that this is no place for you. I don't know what he means by that. Watch yourself, Kostik," Sergei said in a hushed voice.

"Thank you, Sergei. That's exactly what I needed to hear. One more thing...did Smitty say anything about what Mr. Kolkova might have said?"

Sergei thought for a moment. Again, he looked around. "Yes, Kostik. He said Mr. Kolkova said to him what I just told you. My goodness. You work hard, Kostik. I don't know why they would make you leave."

It was time for the two to go to their work stations. As Kostik turned to go, he spotted Smitty. Instead of going to the rear area of the plant, he walked to where Smitty was standing.

"Good morning, Kostik," said Smitty (who then said in very broken Russian), "How are you?"

Kostik answered in Russian that he was fine and added, "That was good, Smitty. Pretty soon you'll be able to go on a trip to Russia."

"Oh, sure, Kostik. I'm not doing in Russian what you're doing in American."

They both laughed.

"Smitty," said Kostik, "I have to ask something from you."

"Okay, what?"

"Since my American is not good, Sergei said he would translate for me if you don't understand how much I am saying. I need to talk to you maybe after work. Sergei said he would stay."

"You are doing okay, Kostik. Your American is getting better and better. What is it you want to talk to me about?" He saw Kostik looking left and right, acting quite nervous. "Just say it, Kostik," Smitty said in a reassuring voice which Kostik appreciated. "Would you feel better if we went into my office and closed the door?"

"Da, da – yes, yes," answered Kostik.

The other workers watched the two of them. Quietly, they started "spinning" a story – actually several stories, none of which, of course, was true; but, the men chose bits and pieces of the stories. They tried to put the pieces together, but no one could come up with any definitive line. Smitty's office was all glass around three sides, so he could see out and all out could see in. Smitty saw the group standing outside and raised his right arm with his hand made into a fist. He motioned – strongly – for the men to move on. They did.

Kostik began to tell Smitty what he was thinking of doing. It took a while to get the whole story – or at least the beginning – out in his broken American. He began perspiring which Smitty could see.

"Wait, Kostik. Relax. I think I know what you are trying to tell me, but why don't we get Sergei in here," offered Smitty.

Kostik nodded yes. Smitty went to the door and told one of the workers to get Rostopovich.

Sergei came to the door and waited to be invited in. "For cryin' out loud, Sergei, come in and close the door," Smitty yelled. "Sit down." When Sergei was seated, Smitty told Kostik to start now.

Kostik said several things, making sure Sergei got it all. This went on for an hour. Kostik looked at Sergei and furtively at Smitty to catch his facial expressions. He could detect neither anger nor...he could detect nothing.

"Okay, Kostik. Okay, Sergei. I understand. It's time you guys get back to work," said Smitty, his hands on his desk, folded together. He continued staring at his hands.

Kostik and Sergei looked at Smitty, not initially moving. After what seemed like a year to Kostik, he elbowed Sergei and backed to the door. They slipped through the open door, said nothing to Smitty, closed the door and walked quickly away.

"My goodness, Kostik. Are you crazy? You have a good job here. What for you want to do this thing?"

"Yes, Sergei. It sounds crazy to me too, but I don't see what this job has to offer me for the rest of my life. I know I can learn more. I know I can do more. The only way to find out is to try it."

"What do you think Smitty will do and say to Mr. Kolkova, and what will Mr. Kolkova say to you?"

"I can only wait and see, Sergei."

A week went by. Smitty continued to be friendly with Kostik. Saturday was the last day of the work-week. Kostik said to himself that Mr. Kolkova wasn't coming this week. Well, maybe next week. But, Kostik, working in the rear of the plant did not see Mr. Kolkova enter the building and go into Smitty's office.

Smitty told Mr. Kolkova what Kostik had said earlier in the week and that he had Rostopovich do some translating. He further complimented Kostik's American.

"Get Kostik in here, Smitty," Mr. Kolkova said.

Smiling, Smitty told Mr. Kolkova to expect Kostik to be nervous. "You'll see the sweat blossom on his forehead."

"He is a good young man, Smitty, and I can certainly appreciate what his vision is."

Kostik knocked on the door. Smitty told him that Mr. Kolkova wanted to speak to him, and Smitty just sent Kostik to the office without him.

"Hello, Mr. Kolkova. Smitty told me you wanted to see me. I want to talk with you, also," Kostik spoke first.

"Yes, Kostik, Smitty told me about your talk with him."

"Mr. Kolkova, I don't know what to say to you. You have been so good to me, and I feel very guilty..."

Kolkova cut Kostik off. "You don't have to feel guilty about anything. I know what you were going to say, Kostik. My son, I am very proud of you. You remind me of myself a number of years ago. Kostik, I knew you would not stay here. It was only a matter of time. What you were going to tell me I did because of you." Mr. Kolkova emphasized the word 'because'. "Yes, Kostik, because of you. You are a very different young man. I was told what your friends did to – and with – you at Vasili's bar, and I waited to see what you were going to do. You did not disappoint me."

"I don't know what you mean," answered Kostik.

"I'm quite sure you haven't been back to Vasili's bar and I'm just as sure you are not going to. Now, tell me what it is you want to do and who it is you are talking with?"

Kostik started at the beginning, telling him how he had learned about Gorelick and how he searched for and found him. He told Mr. Kolkova what Gorelick has offered him. When Kostik reached the point of where he felt the story ended, he apologized to Kolkova for the time he had taken from the job and for the time he had taken from Kolkova.

"I didn't want to hear all this. I could have stopped you, but I know there is much more and I want to hear it all; for example, what mind-set and time frame are you in all of this?" asked Kolkova.

"I don't understand, Mr. Kolkova," Kostik answered, shrugging his shoulders and shaking his head.

Kolkova smiled, put his hand on Kostik's shoulder and said, "Tell me, Kostik, where are you? You must be asking yourself many questions and every question is pushing you into a brick wall and many times into the brick wall causes you fear, makes you question yourself, maybe you can't do this, maybe you should not even think about something like this."

Kostik looked down at the floor, tilted his head, looked at Kolkova and back again at the floor. His eyes began to well up because Kolkova had struck a nerve. Kolkova knew exactly what he was feeling and thinking, and he also knew he didn't know how to say it to Kolkova.

Kolkova recognized Kostik's discomfort and quickly thought of a way to allay his thoughts. "Let me tell you something, Kostik. What you have been telling me I could have told you. Instead of Kostik Kopituk, I could have said Josef Kolkova is telling you this story and, Kostik, you're going through it twice. How much of what you're saying did you say before you finally said I am going to America? Did you ask yourself the same kind of questions you're now asking? The difference between you coming here and me coming is this:

I was brought here by my father and mother. You came alone. I had more of a foundation right from the beginning. But, Kostik, I'm going to try to build some of that foundation for you. Now, when are you going to start with Gorelick? Has that been talked about?"

"Andy is leaving that up to me," offered Kostik.

"Well, then, what are you thinking?"

"I want to get started with him, but I need..." He cut himself off. He did not want it to sound like he was asking Kolkova for anything.

"Yes, Kostik, what do you need?" Kolkova asked, knowing why Kostik stopped in mid-thought.

"Do you know anything about banks, checking accounts, savings and loans?"

"No, nothing," Kostik answered, almost in a whisper.

"You're going to be using tools. How will you get them to your job site? And, even before that, do you know what kind of tools you're going to need?" said Kolkova. "Do you have any money to buy tools?"

Kostik looked straight into Kolkova's eyes. He steadied his gaze and quickly looked down at the floor, back up again and quickly back down. "I don't have the answer for any of your questions," said Kostik with a tremble in his voice. "Until this moment, I did not realize how unready I am to move. How foolish I...." Kostik is cut off again.

"Foolish is a state of mind, Kostik. You start to think like that and you might as well not think any more of what you are trying to do. Why? Because you are quitting before you even start to lay in your first cement block for a cellar," said Kolkova, his voice raising in anger slightly. "Now, I have a suggestion. I think you should go talk to someone in a bank. You need enough cash set aside in the bank to draw out when you need it. For right now, I think that five thousand dollars is more than enough. I want you to go to Broad Street Central Home Trust Company. Ask to see a man named Henry Louizeaux. I will talk with him tomorrow to tell him you're coming. He will know you don't know much about banking. Okay, Kostik, I wish you the very best in this new venture in your life." Kolkova took Kostik's hand in his, pulled Kostik to him to give him a hug. With that, Kolkova turned and strode quickly away and out of the tannery. He wanted no one to see his eye tearing.

Several days passed before Kostik felt he had his words in their correct place enough for him not to embarrass himself. He told Smitty what he was going to do and asked for time off the next day to go to the bank Mr. Kolkova recommended.

"Good luck, Kostik. I'll be waiting to hear – and so will all the other guys," said Smitty. "So will all the other guys." Smitty's voice almost broke.

CHAPTER TWENTY-FIVE

Kostik slept fitfully. At the first sign of sunrise, he was ready to get out of bed. He had the night before laid out the clothes he would wear to the Broad Street Central Trust Company, the bank Mr. Kolkova told him to go to. He made sure he had the piece of paper Mr. Kolkova had written the banker's name on and placed it carefully in his jacket pocket. He dressed slowly, repeatedly going over in his mind what he wanted to say and how he was going to say it.

"Enough," he said to himself. "I have to get going." He left the bedroom and went to the kitchen where Eugenia was already waiting.

"Good morning, Kostik. You look very nice. You're going to meet with the man Mr. Kolkova told you about?" Eugenia asked.

"Yes, I have been practicing what I am going to say. I just hope I can remember everything I want to say."

Kostik spoke well. His accent was fairly heavy, but people were usually able to understand him. His use of American words was on occasion hesitant; however, he did well even though he had spoken this new language for only three years.

"I wish my American was better, so I could talk better with the people I'm meeting today. Mr. Kolkova said they are good people, but I am still a little scared."

"Kostik, my gosh. You have had more hard things that you have faced before this. You know what you want, you know what you don't want, and I think you can explain the difference very good. I bet Mr. Kolkova already has said something about that. He thinks you are very smart and probably told them that. They will listen to him because he has done very good for himself coming from nothing to where he is. You are like him, Kostik," Eugenia said to Kostik.

Kostik was embarrassed and his face turned a little more red. "I believe you are surer of me than I am, Eugenia."

"Now, don't make me mad, Kostik. You know you can do what you set your mind to. You've already done that – many times over. I don't want to hear that kind of talk from you. I've told you that before. Next time, I'm going to slap you," Eugenia raised her voice and shook her finger at Kostik, but she started to smile and so did Kostik. He got up and went to Eugenia to hug her. They had almost a true mother/son relationship.

"I have got to go, Eugenia. I have to ask the trolley driver where this bank is and I want to get there early. I don't want to look like a greenhorn."

"Kostik, slow down. You are making me nervous. You will do all right, I promise. You will. Now go."

Kostik walked quickly to the trolley stop. He asked the trolley driver if he knew where the bank was. He said he did and would tell Kostik when to get off. Kostik fidgeted all the way to his stop and almost tripped as he rushed through the bus doorway.

The trolley driver yelled to Kostik to be careful. Kostik turned, waved, smiled and strode quickly toward where the driver pointed.

"Well, here I am," Kostik said to himself. "I will do all right. Didn't Eugenia say I would?" He laughed to himself.

As he entered the bank, a young man asked him for whom he was looking. Kostik told him he was looking for Mr. Louizeaux. Thanking him, Kostik walked to the office stopping at the doorway. Mr. Louizeaux looked up to see Kostik standing in the entrance.

"Good morning. May I help you," he said to Kostik.

"Yes sir, Mr. Louizeaux. I am Kostik Kopituk. Mr. Kolkova said I should come to talk with you."

"Ah, yes. He told me a bit about you and spoke highly of you. Please come in and have a seat right here," he said to Kostik and pointed to a chair in front of his desk."

Obviously nervous, he bumped into the chair and sat down hard.

Mr. Louizeaux recognized how nervous Kostik was and started the conversation about the fine weather they were having.

This took Kostik completely off-guard. What did the weather have to do with why he was there?

"I don't understand, Mr. Louizeaux. What...."

"No, no, Mr. Kopituk. I just noticed how nervous you were, and I was trying to temporarily get your mind off why you were here. Maybe talking about the weather, something you could easily talk about, would get you somewhat more comfortable. Please, we are not from Czarist Russia," he said with a grin.

Kostik grinned and then laughed. "All right, Mr. Louizeaux, you did very good. I think I'm not as scared anymore. Thank you."

"Well, Mr. Kopituk, tell me about yourself. Where are you from, how did you decide to come to America, how old are you, where did you get the money to come to America? Answers to all these questions should be a good start."

Kostik started with the first question. Mr. Louizeaux interrupted with a few questions, but let Kostik tell his whole story. He talked for three hours.

"I think I've got a fairly good picture of you, Mr. Kopituk," said Mr. Louizeaux, smiling.

"I don't understand. When did you take my picture?" Kostik asked.

"No, no, Mr. Kopituk. That's just an expression meaning I have learned a lot about you. Your story is really interesting. You have done a great deal in your young life, and I admire how you have handled your life up to now. And now, Mr. Kopituk, let's get to why you are here – at my bank."

"Mr. Kolkova has been very good to me, and I feel bad to leave him but what his company does doesn't really interest me. I don't see me doing what I am doing all the rest of my life, and so, I have someone from my village in Russia who said he would teach me what he does."

"And what is that, Mr. Kopituk?" Mr. Louizeaux interrupted.

"He is a carpenter. He repairs houses, builds porches. If I can learn to do those things, I can maybe do more in just a few years."

"What is it that you think you would like to do in a few years? Have you given that any thought?" Mr. Louizeaux smiled to himself. Several years later he would tell Kostik he already knew the answer to his question.

"Yes, I think I would like to buy land and build houses," said Kostik very matter-of-factually.

Mr. Louizeaux said nothing. He looked at Kostik pridefully and thought to himself: This young man will do it, too. All I have to do is help him financially as much as I can and as much as this bank can.

"As I said earlier, Mr. Kopituk, why are you here? You have told me what you would like to do, but what does that have to do with me and/or this bank?"

95

Kostik had never been taught the rules of negotiation, the rules of tact and diplomacy in this type of situation. Without hesitation, Kostik answered Mr. Louizeaux in a very straight-forward manner, leaving no room for equivocation: "You are going to give me the money to get me started, Mr. Louizeaux. Why else do you think I would be here?"

"I couldn't think of any other reason, Kostik – may I call you Kostik, Mr. Kopituk?

"Of course, call me Kostik," he answered. "I am sorry I didn't tell you sooner."

"All right, Kostik, what are you going to buy and how much is it going to cost?" Mr. Louizeaux got the financial question started.

Kostik had no idea how much to ask for. He knew he had to buy tools, but he did not know exactly what kind of tolls he would need. He would have to go to Gorelick to find out. He chastised himself for not having that information and apologized to Mr. Louizeaux. He thanked Mr. Louizeaux for his time and said he was going to talk to Gorelick about the equipment he would need.

Kostik left the bank and immediately caught the next trolley to Gorelick's house.

Gorelick told Kostik not to buy tools now. He should use his tools until he earned enough to buy his own. That way he would not have to borrow as much from the bank.

"When do you want to start working with me, Kostik?"

"As soon as possible, Andy, but I have to tell Mr. Kolkova I am ready to leave his company."

"All right, Kostik. You can start with me anytime."

The next day, Kostik went to the tannery the next day. He asked Smitty if he knew when Mr. Kolkova was coming. Smitty told Kostik he would contact Mr. Kolkova and tell him that Kostik wanted to talk with him.

Kostik worked at the tannery until Mr. Kolkova came. He told Mr. Kolkova about Mr. Louizeaux and about what Gorelick had said.

"When do you plan to start with Gorelick?" asked Mr. Kolkova.

"I think as soon as you say I can stop working here," Kostik answered.

"You can leave anytime you would like, Kostik. I cannot hold you back. I am sorry to see you leave, but I fully understand. I'm sure you want to say goodbye to all the men here. Go ahead, do that. I'll say goodbye now and wish you luck. I know in my heart you will be successful in anything you do. I will be seeing you from time to time and watching your progress."

The two shook hands and hugged each other. As they pulled away from each other, Mr. Kolkova handed Kostik twenty-five dollars, turned and walked away. Kostik was very surprised. He watched Mr. Kolkova leave the building. Then he looked for Sergei. After Kostik thanked Sergei for all his help, the two said their goodbyes. Kostik then found Smitty and thanked him for all he had done for him. Kostik spoke to a few of the other men and then left the plant.

CHAPTER TWENTY-SIX

Kostik felt very good about his new venture now that it appeared it would become a reality.

"Tomorrow I begin another new life," Kostik told himself. "I have to be ready. Andy is giving me a big chance, and I have to listen close to everything he tells me — and remember what he tells me, s I have to get a good night's sleep so I'll be ready in the morning."

Gorelick showed Kostik where he was to sleep. "I'll wake you about six in the morning, Kostik. We'll have some breakfast and then go to the job."

"I'll be ready, Andy. I'll probably be awake anyway. I don't know if I'm going to be able to sleep."

Kostik was almost correct. He twisted and turned, first on his back, then on his stomach, then on one side or the other. Finally, his mind gave up — or maybe his body, or maybe both at the same time. The next thing Kostik knew was Andy shaking him awake. He leaped out of bed, telling Andy he would be ready in five minutes. Andy laughed and left the room.

After breakfast, Andy and Kostik rode to Andy's job site in his truck. Quickly, Kostik reached for an apron which held several tools, handed one to Andy and wrapped one around his own waist. The house they were to work on was almost completed; the front porch was what Andy had to construct. The foundation and pedestals were already in place. The tongue and groove boards for the flooring were stacked neatly in front of the house, some sixteen feet in length, some twelve feet in length. Andy explained how the boards would be used and told Kostik to get a saw from the truck and start cutting the boards to their correct lengths.

"Before we start laying the floor, Kostik, we have to make sure that we have correct shims to be placed under the boards. Why do you think we have to use these shims, Kostik?"

"To make sure the floor is level," Kostik answered. If wrong, Andy would explain and/or show in detail. Andy's use of this method of teaching was showing effective results.

Kostik caught on fairly quickly. After several repetitious jobs, Andy told Kostik what had to be done and Andy let Kostik go without watching him. That pleased Kostik. As the jobs became more intricate, Kostik asked more questions and Andy didn't mind because he knew Kostik was mastering more aspects of the building trade.

The time came for Kostik to ask Andy to take him to buy a horse and wagon. "How much money do you have, Kostik?" Andy asked.

"I don't believe I have enough, so I will go to Louizeaux and borrow what I don't got. That's why I need to go someplace that sells horses and find the cost of what I need."

"All right, Kostik. We'll go tomorrow."

Kostik told the man at the horse stable that he needed a workhorse and one that was not very expensive. He explained to the man what the animal was to be used for.

"You starting your own business?" the man asked.

"No, not yet. I am working for this man now, but maybe sometime later on, I will start my own," said Kostik.

"He will, too," offered Andy. "This young fellow is smart and a good worker. I will do all I can to help him get started."

"That's very nice," said the man. "He is lucky that he has someone to show him the ropes. Let's go look at a horse. I also have a few wagons that should be good for what he needs."

The three men walked into the stalls. They walked past several and as they came to the eighth one, the man stopped.

"I think this might be your horse, young man. He is one of my quietest and will pull your wagon easily," the man told Kostik. "He is about six years old, and I don't ever recall him being sick. He eats good, and I'll give you what and how much you need to feed him."

"Let's take him out of the stall," said Andy. "Put him in the fenced area and see how he runs."

The man did what Andy wanted. Then Andy asked him if he could bring a person who knows horses to look at him. The man agreed without hesitation. Andy turned his back to the man, looked directly at Kostik and nodded his head, almost imperceptibly.

"How much you will sell this horse?" Kostik asked.

"How old are you, young man? What is your name?" the man asked.

"I am almost twenty years. My name is Kostik."

"Well, Kostik, I'm going to do something I don't do often. When I have done it, it turned out that I have not been wrong yet. I think you are going to do okay. So, I am going to sell this horse for less than I would usually sell him for. I think you will treat him good, be a good friend to him, and I believe you are going to do good yourself. Instead of the ninety dollars, I'll let you have him for seventy. Can you pay that?" the man asked.

Kostik looked at Andy who said, "Let's see what the wagon is going to cost."

The salesman said that he didn't think Kostik would need a two-horse wagon which is about twice the price of a one-horse wagon.

"I'll work with you on a wagon, too," he said. "I've got one outside here. Let's go look."

The wagon was just the right size for what Kostik would need. He could carry his tools and the lumber he needed for small jobs once Andy let him go off on his own.

"This looks good," said Kostik. "What do you think, Andy?" Andy was already looking at the bed, the axles, the tailgate and sides, to detect rotting wood or any other problems.

"I really don't see anything wrong with it, Kostik," said Andy. "How much do you want for it?" he asked the man.

"How about thirty-three dollars?" the man answered.

"I think you should get the money, Kostik," Andy said.

"I have to go to the bank," said Kostik to the salesman. "I will be back tomorrow."

The next day Kostik went to see Mr. Louizeaux. He explained what he had been doing since they last talked.

"And now you need money to buy things to further your career goals. Is that right, Kostik?" Mr. Louizeaux said.

"Yes, I think so," Kostik answered. "A horse."

Hesitantly, Mr. Louizeaux asked, "You need to buy...a... what?"

"A horse. He will pull the wagon you are also going to help me buy," Kostik said quickly.

Mr. Louizeaux laughed. He enjoyed Kostik's self-assuredness, his lack of hesitation in showing what he wanted done and his leaving no room for questioning.

Kostik, too, began to laugh. After all, he thought to himself, it is what I need, I need it now and what is wrong with saying it.

"All right, Kostik, how much are we – am I (Louizeaux corrected himself and emphasized "I") - going to have to spend?" Louizeaux asked with a lilt in his voice. He did enjoy this young man very much.

"Seventy dollars for the horse and thirty-three for the wagon."

"Have you seen the horse and wagon or are you guessing how much they cost?"

"No, I already know how much, but I'm going to talk some more. The guy I talk to already came down, so I don't know if he comes some more down."

"Sounds like you're doing all right, Kostik. I'll loan you the money. When do you want it?"

"Now," Kostik answered. "I will go tomorrow with Gorelick and buy."

CHAPTER TWENTY-SEVEN

The next day Andy and Kostik bought the horse and wagon. The man put a bale of hay and a big bag of oats and a feed bag on the wagon bed. Since Kostik knew where he was going to keep the horse and wagon, he and Andy went there.

"Now, I have to get to and from work and have to carry my tools – but I don't have the tools... Tell me, Andy, what tools I am going to need right away. I hope Mr. Louizeaux is going to give me money for them."

"Kostik, I'll tell you something. He will give you the money. You are too young to see it, but you are going to get anything you want from that man."

"What do you mean?" Kostik asked, not understanding what Gorelick was saying.

"Kostik, he has taken you in like you are his son, he is acting proud of you, and he wants to make sure you will succeed. He is going to help you to get where you want to go. I wish I had someone like that to be behind me. The thing is, Kostik, he knows that whatever money he loans you, you are going to pay him back. I don't know what you have done for him to think of you as he does but whatever it is, don't do anything to mess it up."

"What do I do, Andy? I don't...."

"Just don't think about it, Kostik. I think all you need to do is to be yourself. You're a good kid, Kostik...don't change."

Kostik hugged him. Andy said, "All right, Kostik, let's go to Sears and Roebuck and see what kind of tools they have."

They put together a list of what Andy thought he would need to get started and Kostik wrote down the price of each tool. They went directly to the bank.

The next day Andy went to the site of Kostik's first job on his own. The customer wanted a white fence all around the house with a swinging gate at the front. He took the measurements, listed the hardware he needed and went to the lumber yard to get the materials.

"I have to open an account with your company," Kostik told the manager of the yard.

"How are you going to pay for the materials?" the manager asked Kostik in a somewhat harsh tone of voice.

"I have a letter from Mr. Louizeaux at the Broad Street Central Bank," said Kostik as he handed the letter to the manager. The letter stated that Kostik had an account at the bank with sufficient funds to cover the materials he would be buying from the lumber yard. The manager took the document, told Kostik to wait at the counter and went into his office where he called Mr. Louizeaux.

"All right young man, let's load your wagon. Mr. Louizeaux said to give you what you want. If he says so, that's good enough for me."

CHAPTER TWENTY-EIGHT

Kostik unloaded his wagon and laid out his lumber in neat stacks. His first task was to construct a pair of saw horses so he could cut the lumber as needed. Completing that, he decided he would cut all of the lumber into the correct sizes required, stack in neat piles the different sized pieces and then paint each piece with two coats of white paint. By the time he had finished the first coat, the paint had dried so that the second could be applied. When that was accomplished, Kostik was very excited to begin building the fence.

As he built the fence, Kostik took great care in measurements, making certain the boarders were exactly the same height and the slats were spaced the same. He was meticulous. He developed a rule which he followed almost to the letter: "Measure ten times, nail it in place once." His first major job on his own took an inordinate amount of time, but he made no mistakes, nothing had to be redone. However, he slowly reduced his measurements to a "livable" number.

His last walk-around the job was to see there were no smudges, marks or scratches on any of the white paint. He carried a paint bucket and brush to touch up any missed area that he found. As he came around a corner from the back of the house to the front, he could not believe what he saw. Standing on his swinging gate was a young girl swinging as if she were testing to see if it truly was a swinging gate. It was working as he hoped it would.

In a loud, unfriendly, threatening voice, Kostik yelled, "Hey, you, little girl, get off that gate. What do you think you are doing?!!?" As he yelled, he ran toward her, pulled his hammer from his apron and threw it at her. Frightened, the girl jumped from the gate and ran from the yard. Kostik did not follow. He was more interested in seeing what damage her shoes had done to his painted gate. The paint was slightly scuffed but no serious damage was done. Two slaps of the brush were sufficient to repair the smudges.

Shortly after Kostik finished the gate, the owner of the house came by.

"It looks like the fence is finished, and it really looks good," the man said to Kostik.

"Come, let us walk along the whole fence and see if the work I did was what you expected." Kostik shook hands with the homeowner.

The two walked slowly, looking over all the posts and fencing. "Mr. Kopituk, you have done very good work. I know my wife will be very happy."

"Thank you. I am happy about that, but I was unhappy about some little girl who was using the gate for a swing. I don't know what house she ran to. Would you happen to know her?" Kostik asked.

"Yes, her name is Anna Krawczyk and she's visiting from Scotch Plains. She's a sweet little nine-year-old. She was born in Poland and came here when she was about six months old."

"Well, I don't like her," Kostik said with a smile. "You tell her to stay off my gate. It is not for swinging."

"I'll tell her. Well, let me pay you. I take it you agreed to do the work for what Mr. Gorelick told me."

"Yes. Is everything all right?" asked Kostik.

"Oh, very much all right. In fact, I am going to pay you a little bit more. I am very pleased with your work."

"Thank you very much. Please tell your friends." Kostik climbed aboard his wagon and drove off.

CHAPTER TWENTY-NINE

Kostik worked with Gorelick for several months on a variety of jobs, all of which helped Kostik learn more about carpentry.

"Kostik, do you think you can put a porch on a house?" Andy asked.

"I don't know, Andy. What do you think? Do you think I can?" Kostik asked nervously.

"No, Kostik, you tell me. If I am going to give you the job, I don't want to hear you ask me if I think you can. The question is, do you think so? But, I want you to tell me 'yes, I can' or 'no, I can't'. Which is it Kostik?" Andy was not making it easy for Kostik. Andy knew he could, but he wanted Kostik to make himself believe he could – even if he had to force himself a little bit.

Kostik looked directly at Andy. "I will do it," he said, "Where is it?"

"I'll take you there," said Andy.

Kostik was initially frightened by the enormity of the project, an enormity for someone who had never built one before. A trench had to be dug because the porch was going to need a foundation. Kostik would be able to use the bricklaying skills he learned in Russia. If he hadn't forgotten them.

"Andy, how big is this porch supposed to be? Did you discuss this with the people who own this house?"

"No, Kostik, I did not. You and I are going to discuss it together with the owners. I am going to let you talk with them. Find out what they want and write down as much as you can. I will be here to add things that you may not know so write down what I say, too. But you are going to get all the material prices and prepare an estimate for the people. You need to do that pretty quick to present it to them. I'll help you."

"Andy, I am going to need some help. Can I use some of the men you use?"

"Sure, Kostik, but remember you're going to have to start keeping a ledger on what you're spending, who you're paying and how much. What day are you going to choose for paying your men? That has to be the same every week. In fact, Kostik, I would recommend you hire somebody to keep your records. You're going to have enough to do without having to worry about keeping your records straight."

"Do you have someone like that, Andy," Kostik asked. "How much do you pay him? Could I use him?"

"Yes, I have a bookkeeper. No, I don't think you could use him, Kostik. He already has several people he.....well, wait a minute. That's for him to say yes or no. I'll ask him, Kostik, but before I do, I would suggest you talk to Louizeaux. He could certainly get you started."

The next day Kostik took the trolley to the bank. As usual, Henry was glad to see Kostik.

"What's the project I'm going to have to pay for today, Kostik? It has been a while since I've seen you. I assume you have something I'm going to have to pay for," Mr. Louizeaux said with a laugh.

Kostik told Louizeaux what he had facing him. Louizeaux was grinning from ear to ear.

"Kostik, you are on your way. Now let's talk about how you're going to keep track of your money. You say you're going to have to hire some men?" Louizeaux asked, "How many?"

"I think I will start with two and I think I will need to hire somebody to do book-work. Do you know somebody I could hire?"

The two men spent several hours setting Kostik up with a checking account, a payroll account and enough cash to get each account ready to be useable. Kostik's head was swimming.

"Kostik, you look lost," Louizeaux said softly. He knew that this was a huge leap for Kostik. He hoped that Gorelick realized what must be going through Kostik's mind and that he would give support. He thought he would talk to Gorelick about that.

Kostik prepared the estimate he would give to the homeowner, but first he had Andy look at it. Andy made only a few changes in the presentation.

"Kostik, this is very good. Are you sure you have never done this before? This is really your first one?"

"Well, Andy, I guess I am ready to get started. Tomorrow I will lay out the foundation measurements and have the men dig the trench for the concrete."

Kostik placed the stakes in the ground and hung the string that would be the guide for the brick wall of the foundation he had planned. The men he hired followed Kostik's instructions and did not hesitate to ask questions if they did not understand what he wanted. Kostik spoke in English. Fortunately, the two Russian men he hired had been in America for many years and had learned the American language well enough to understand it. When they did not, Kostik would then slip into Russian to explain what he wanted. He thought to himself that this was going to work out well. Since the two were experienced carpenters, they were a tremendous help in the actual building of the porch and offered suggestions that made Kostik appreciate them even more. He realized that these two men were invaluable and definitely should be kept as employees of the small company he was forming.

The two men were familiar with bricklaying, but Kostik's expertise surprised them. Kostik soon noticed they were not comfortable building the brick foundation wall. He stopped the work to show them how best to lay the bricks. They thanked him for teaching them again and he reciprocated by telling them he was pleased with their work. This was the beginning of a good bond between boss and employee.

CHAPTER THIRTY

Several weeks into the building of the porch, Kostik ran into a snag. The porch roof had to attach to the house roof and look like it had always been one roof. The two men, Nicholas and Nikita, had some ideas but they were not sure. Kostik studied the situation using the ideas of the two men plus his own ingenuity until he was almost convinced the ideas were correct. That night he talked with Andy who said he would come by first thing in the morning.

With only a few changes, Andy told Kostik and the two men their idea would work but it wasn't strong enough. The roof would need a few additional rafters. Andy showed them what had to be done, and it was an easy change.

Kostik was very pleased with how well this project was going. He was also happy Stanley Slovinski, the man he had hired as his bookkeeper. He quickly caught on to the way Stanley moved the money around from one account to another. Henry Louizeaux was pleased with how well the person he had recommended was working out and liked the way he set up the books for Kostik.

The porch project finished without any further snags, but now Kostik and his men were without work. A friend of Andy's was building houses for speculation and Andy told him about Kostik and the two men. He convinced his friend to hire the three men. This was exactly what Kostik was hoping for. The job would last over a year and give Kostik time to learn about building houses from the ground up. In fact, things were going so well the builder decided to keep building "spec" houses.

The first world war in Europe seemed to be winding down. Soldiers would be coming home, getting married, having families and would need places to live. This could not have been better for Kostik. He was earning good money. Therefore, he decided he could afford a truck to replace his horse and wagon.

That night he talked with Andy about buying a Ford truck. Andy told Kostik he would take him to the dealership tomorrow. The next morning, they drove to the Hersh Motor Car Company showroom in Elizabeth and looked at the trucks the dealership had in stock. Kostik wanted a small truck but didn't know trucks were sized by the weight they would carry: half-ton, three-quarter-ton, one-ton, etc. What Kostik would need, he would learn, would be a half-ton.

"Good morning," a salesman said as he approached Kostik. "I see you are looking at trucks. What size do you need?"

"Good morning. Yes, I am looking to buy a pickup truck. I see many here in your yard. This is the first time I am buying a truck, so I don't know what size I need."

Kostik explained how he was going to use the truck.

"Okay. I think I know what size truck would work for you," said the salesman. He told Kostik his name was David, got Kostik's name and began explaining the different sized trucks. "For what you're going to use the truck, you don't need anything bigger than a half-ton. Let me show you some that we have." David began to walk toward the trucks. "What are you driving now, Kostik?" he asked.

"A horse and wagon," Kostik answered which stunned David.

"A horse and a wagon," David repeated slowly.

"Yes, I would be happy to sell both to you – or maybe I could trade them for one of your trucks," Kostik spoke with a straight face.

David hesitated. He wasn't sure if Kostik were serious. "No, Kostik, I'm sorry. I don't think they would really fit into our operation," David said with a smile. "What are you going to do with them?"

"I have to sell them," answered Kostik. "Do you know anybody who might want a horse and wagon?"

"No, but I'll ask around for you," said David.

"I'm sorry, Kostik, but I have to ask you: if you decide you want to buy one of our trucks, how will you pay for it?"

"I will pay in cash," answered Kostik without hesitation.

"You have that much money?" David asked with a tone of disbelief.

Kostik caught the tone and was not pleased with it. "Yes, I do. Do you think I am not able to have so much?" Kostik said with a little harshness in his voice.

"Well, it would not be the first time a man came in to buy a truck and when he was told the price, would only have half the amount required," David answered.

"I am not one of those men," Kostik shot back.

"Kostik, I'm sorry. I did not mean to insult you," said David, "but I do get some that come in here who are like that."

Kostik did not respond. He walked to one of the trucks and got in. "Tell me, David, I see that truck next to this one is the same as this one. Is the price for this one the same as the price for that one?"

"No, Kostik, this one costs a little more."

"Why?" asked Kostik.

"It has better seat covers, two tail-lights instead of the usual one and a windshield rain wiper. You have to operate the wiper manually but for a couple of dollars more, you can take that truck over there which is the same as this one except it has an electric wiper so you don't have to take your hands off the steering wheel."

"I will buy that one," Kostik quickly decided. "What do you think, Andy?"

"Good choice, Kostik," answered Andy.

Kostik gave David a down-payment and then he and Andy went to the stable where he had purchased the horse and wagon. That business would buy back the two but at a reduced price. Kostik agreed and asked if they could pick up the horse and wagon. They could but would charge an additional fee. Kostik agreed.

Andy drove Kostik to the bank. "You must have bought a truck, Kostik," Mr. Louizeaux said as Kostik entered Mr. Louizeaux's office. How much is it going to cost me?" Kostik and Louizeaux laughed. They both agreed to the cost of the truck would deplete most of the money in Kostik's accounts. Therefore, Mr. Louizeaux added money to Kostik's checking account to cover the cost of the truck and maintain the balance in his other accounts.

"Don't worry, Kostik," Louizeaux said. "You are not going to break the bank. It has more money than you will ever need. If you deplete your other accounts, we can provide additional funds"

Kostik shook his head. "I am scared but I am happy – all at the same time. I thank you, Mr. Louizeaux, for everything you have done and are doing for me. I want you to know that."

"You just do more of what you're doing, Kostik. I – and everybody here at the bank – are proud of you. We are very glad to have you as a client."

Andy and Kostik went back to the dealership to get Kostik's truck. Andy drove off and Kostik went in to get his truck. It had been quite some time since Kostik had seen Eugenia; he drove to her home.

CHAPTER THIRTY-ONE

Kostik had learned a great deal working for Andy's friend. It wasn't long before Kostik became the foreman for the man building the "spec" houses. He learned what lumber to order, when and how much; when to start wiring, and plumbing. He began taking notes pertaining to the sequences of construction which he discussed with Nikita and Nicholas. The three were becoming a good team which Kostik appreciated. His plan for the future was solidifying. He took care not to become over-confident, not to get beyond what he thought he could handle. In another year, he would be ready.

The time was approaching when Kostik thought he would strike out on his own. Each evening and on weekends, he drove around the city of Elizabeth looking for good parcels of land that were for sale or the owner might be persuaded to sell.

On one of his searches, he came upon a large undeveloped tract that already had a road built its full length. I will go see Mr. Louizeaux tomorrow.

"What am I buying now, Kostik?" Mr. Louizeaux greeted Kostik as he walked through the office door.

Kostik laughed and said one word, "land."

"Land. You're serious. What kind of land?"

"Come with me, Mr. Louizeaux. I want to show it to you."

"All right, I'll go with you. Is this one lot or bigger than one lot?"

"It is bigger," answered Kostik.

"It's in Elizabeth?"

"Yes, sir."

They drove for about ten minutes. When they came to the land, all Kostik said was, "There it is," and pointed to the right side of the truck's hood and waved his hand farther down the street in the direction the truck was headed.

"This whole thing, Kostik?" Henry asked incredulously. "You want to buy this whole piece, Kostik? What are you planning?"

"I build houses," Kostik answered. "Two-story houses and maybe small stores."

"Do you know how to build a two-story house, Kostik? Where did you learn to do that?"

"I know how," answered Kostik, smiling. "How long you have known me, Mr. Louizeaux? You know I do nothing until I know what to do."

"I know, Kostik, I know. I know, but this is a huge undertaking. You're looking at thousands, tens of thousands of dollars, possibly hundreds of thousands!"

"Thousands that you are going to give me." Kostik looked directly at Henry.

"How much is this land, Kostik – and who owns it now?"

"I need you to help me find the owner and tell me the architect you want me to use." (Kostik didn't pronounce the 'ch' as a 'k' in architect but as a 'ch' in chicken).

"Let's go back to the bank, Kostik."

On the drive back to the bank, Henry Louizeaux kept silent. Kostik became concerned. Is this project too big for the bank to lend me the money to get it started? Does Mr. Louizeaux think that I am not capable of doing the project?

Back in the bank, the two men sat in Henry's office.

"Kostik, I have watched you for several years. You have always amazed me at what you tackle and how well you complete what you start. I have no problem with the amounts of money you have borrowed because you have always paid it back. This project, I have to be honest with you, is huge. I am concerned that you don't, or can't, fully grasp the enormity of the dollar amount. Do you understand what I am saying to you? You have nothing backing you. We call that collateral – something that can be taken from you to pay back the loan if your project fails. Given the amount of the loan, you could be working for many years to pay it back. I know how hard you would work to do so for you would never turn your back on your debt. Do you understand what I am trying to tell you?"

"Yes, I understand, Mr. Louizeaux, but everything you're saying is that I am going to fail. I don't fail. I may make mistake, but I don't fail. How 'bout we do this? I go home and think. You go home and think. I come back tomorrow, and we talk again."

With that, Kostik left the bank, got into his truck and drove back to his project site. There he stopped and sat in his truck until dark, thinking of all the different avenues he could take. At one point, Kostik could feel the tears welling up in his eyes. No, he thought, I will not let this stop me. I will do it. The next morning, he was at the bank when it opened.

CHAPTER THIRTY-TWO

"Mr. Louizeaux, I am going to do it. I will not fail," Kostik said in a very strong – and slightly deepened voice. "I have it – how you call – prop..., prop..."

"Proposition," Henry finished Kostik's sentence. "Come, Kostik, sit down. Close the door, please. What is your proposition?"

Kostik admitted that everything he had done up to this point was very small compared to what he now wanted to do. He knew that Mr. Louizeaux had the bank to think of, not just this young Russian immigrant. Would he help Kostik find the owner of the property?

"That's no problem, Kostik. I can find the owner. Why? What are you thinking?"

"You and I will talk to him or them. We will try to get him to sell enough of the strip of land to build one house. I will give him money for the piece, and a deposit on the entire strip so he will hold it for me before someone else makes an offer. The thing is, will you loan me the money I will need to buy this property, pay for the lumber and the workers I will need. I also have to hire laborers, an electrician, plumber, plasterer and an architect.

"Kostik, I cannot give you an answer today. I am going to have to talk with the other officers of the bank to see what their collective thinking might be."

"When could you talk with them?"

"I know, Kostik. You have thought this out very well and are in a hurry to get started. You _do_ realize this is just the beginning. Please understand this is no simple matter. You have not thought of everything, nor have I in counseling you, I'm sure the other officers will have questions we haven't thought of. I know they will want time to think it over. However, the very first thing we must do is find the owner and talk with him. Right now, we don't know what his plans for the property are."

"How long this will take?" asked Kostik.

"Kostik, I fully understand you are ready to jump in with both feet...."

"What you mean about my feet?"

Mr. Louizeaux smiled. He had to explain to Kostik what that saying meant. Kostik laughed and said he understood. He said he didn't want to jump in and drown; he knew he had to slow down and get solid ground under his feet.

"I will call City Hall, Kostik, and find out who owns that property. I'm hoping that one man owns it all. It'll be easier to deal with. You can sit right there while I call."

After he called City Hall and learned the identity of the owner, Henry Louizeaux told Kostik he would contact the owner and would set up a meeting with him.

CHAPTER THIRTY-THREE

The meeting went well as the owner was very accommodating and understanding of both Kostik's financial needs and goals. A lot at the corner of the property was measured and a price set that would be applicable to each subsequent piece should Kostik's building a house on this lot turn out to be successful.

"Well, Kostik, you are on your way, aren't you?" Henry said.

"Yes, it looks like maybe, but first, I have to pay for land, no?"

"Yes, you do, but much has to be done first."

"Now I have to go to lumber yard and order all the materials I am going to need to get started."

"Aren't you jumping ahead of yourself, Kostik?" asked Mr. Louizeaux.

"What? What do you mean, Mr. Louizeaux?" Kostik asked, surprised at being taken down from his mountaintop.

"I know you are excited and I shouldn't interrupt the grand feeling you have at this moment, but do you have the architect's plans for this house? How do you know what you have to order? How many rooms is this house going to have? How many bathrooms? How big is the kitchen going to be? I could go on, but I think you know what I mean."

Kostik was shaken. He was too intent on looking at the finished picture, and he somehow forgot to put the brush strokes on the canvas. He sat alone, shaking his head.

"How I did that, Mr. Louizeaux?"

"Kostik, do not – I repeat – *do not* be ashamed! You were moving so fast you thought your mountaintop euphoria would last through any problems, big or small. You are young, son, and you have just learned a great lesson.

121

From what I have seen of you, you really do not have much to learn. In all your project, you have planned very well. Just remember this situation."

"I will. What is meaning euph....,eupho...., eupho...something?"

Henry chuckled, said the word, spelled it and gave its definition.

"Euphoria can make you feel wonderful. Just don't allow it to overtake your directions," said Louizeaux.

Kostik walked to Louizeaux, took his hand and shook it strongly. "I owe you much, Mr. Louizeaux, and I don't mean the money you are giving me. I thank you so very much. I will make you proud. Could you please call the architect to see if he has drawings to show to me?"

"He is ready to get with you. He will come to my office tomorrow morning at nine o'clock."

The meeting went very well. Following it, several weeks passed during which Kostik spent a great deal of time with Nicholas, Nikita and the architect. Basically, what he had designed was a fairly good-sized two-story house. Both Nicholas and Nikita talked about how difficult certain parts would be to build and how easy certain other parts would be. The architect was able to make some adjustments which lessened many of the difficulties.

Kostik was grateful for the two young carpenters. Though it was not hands-on learning, Kostik had the capacity to grasp concepts easily which was recognized by both of them and the architect, and they told him so.

"Well, Kostik, what's next?" asked Nicholas.

"You tell me, Nicholas. You, too, Nikita. My head is so full. I don't know where to reach in and pull out what I do next," Kostik said, laughing. I think next we need someone who can clean the land of grass, weeds and other things growing where we will build our first house."

Kostik went to see Andy Gorelick to ask if he knew someone who could clear the land and he said he did. Andy took Kostik to meet Bernie Ozkowski and introduced him. Kostik told him what he needed, and they decided to go to the lot that was to be cleared.

"I can do this, Kostik," Bernie said.

"When you could do it?"

"I can probably do it sometime next week."

Bernie and Kostik sat on the tailgate of Andy's truck to discuss the cost. Kostik asked how much Bernie was going to scrape off; he wanted some ground cover, so the dirt would not change to mud in case of rain. After walking the land that was to be cleared, Kostik and Bernie discussed the price which Kostik thought was too high.

"Now, know this, Bernie, this is the first of a lot of houses I going to build. I going to build this whole block, all the way down to there," Kostik said as he pointed.

"Yeah, Kostik, but you haven't built your first one yet," Bernie answered smiling.

"No, but I am buying the whole block."

"When?" asked Bernie.

"When I finish the first house and sell it," Kostik answered with a little too much testiness in his voice, which Bernie discerned. Kostik was not used to being questioned. He was also not used to negotiating. He had to learn how to conduct himself in a situation such as this. Fortunately, Andy heard what was happening and stepped in.

"Bernie, as you can tell, Kostik is brand new at such a venture as this. Kostik, Bernie is used to doing large jobs. Moving his equipment to clear your one lot will cost him more than clearing the entire block. Do you understand that?" Andy tried to smooth Kostik.

"You think, Andy, that this is good price?" Kostik asked.

Bernie entered the conversation. "Okay, Kostik, I'll tell you what. If I do this job to your satisfaction and you give me the job to do the whole block, I'll do you one lot for free. How's that?

Kostik was embarrassed. He didn't know what to say. He looked at Andy, then at Bernie, then back to Andy.

"That's a pretty good deal, Kostik," said Andy.

"Yes, it is. I am sorry, Bernie, I sounded nasty. I am very sorry. I have lots to learn, don't I?" Kostik said.

"That's okay, Kostik. I was where you are once and I understand. Let's get to work," Bernie said as he offered his hand to shake Kostik's. "This is how I like to do business – with a hand-shake. I'll be back next Tuesday and start clearing this lot," said Bernie as he walked back to his truck.

Kostik went to the bank to tell Henry when and what Bernie Ozkowski was going to do.

CHAPTER THIRTY-FOUR

"Kostik, you have to buy the property before you can do anything on it," Henry said somewhat strongly, yet inwardly he was smiling. He told himself not to be too harsh with this kid, yet he had to be firm. "There is much that has to be done before Ozkowski can do <u>anything</u>." Henry emphasized the word anything. Can you get him and tell him you will be back in touch when all the paperwork and actual purchase is completed?"

"To do what I need to do sounds very complicated," said Kostik softly.

Louizeaux sighed heavily, looked down at his desk and shook his head. Now is as good a time as any to sit this young man down and try to get him to understand that a mad plunge into this project would be very wrong.

"Kostik, I am going to try to give you an idea of what you can and cannot do to and with your project. Right now, if you proceed without a plan of what must be done first, then second, then third and so on, you could kill your project before you even start it. Now, here is a pencil and a pad of paper. I want you to write down a lot of what I am going to tell you. It will take some time, but I will go slowly and repeat when necessary. I know your ability. You will be able to remember much of what I will tell you, but there are things you must get in your head. Don't go off and do something big without asking first. Just think twice before you jump and then think twice again. You will get the idea down before too long." Henry smiled. "Okay, are you ready?"

"Yes, I hope so, Mr. Louizeaux," Kostik answered, very subdued and quiet.

Several weeks passed and virtually all of the legal and other paperwork were completed. The bank approved the property purchase, land clearing and construction loans. When Kostik saw the amount of money the bank was giving him, he for the first time was struck with what to him was the enormity of what he was attempting to do. He started to breathe heavily, rose from his chair and paced back and forth as Henry watched him. "Kostik, calm down. Are you all right? Sit down, son. It is a shock when you see for the first time in your life how much money you'll be responsible for. Keep in mind what I have tried to tell you and good luck. I am here if you need me for anything."

Kostik and Henry shook hands. Kostik left Henry's office shaking his head. Henry had done a very good job in explaining to Kostik how to plan and how to anticipate contingencies. Kostik's apprehension was not yet over-powering, but it was getting close. He noticed his hands shaking. His legs felt like caving. Kostik began talking to himself. "*Do I truly want this? My mind is running a mile a minute! This is absolutely foolish. I cannot do this. No, I cannot do this! So you want to quit? You want to go back to the tannery? Better still, you want to go back to Russia? I had a nice ride across the ocean. I could tell everybody it was just too big for me. I was not ready. I did not quit. I was not ready. Who am I trying to convince? Me? The man down the street?*"

His emotions caught up with him and the flood was greater than the Hudson River. As his eyes filled with tears, he got into his truck and drove to the Arthur Kill, the slice of water between part of eastern New Jersey and western Staten Island where he parked his truck on the bank and shut off the engine. He sat there for over an hour before he drove back to Elizabeth to meet Nicholas and Nikita. When Kostik met with them, the deep concern showed on his face.

"What's wrong, Kostik?" Nicholas was the first to speak. "You don't look good. What happened with the bank? Did they say no to loaning you money?"

"No, the bank gave me money. Mr. Louizeaux talked to me for a long time, explaining – or trying to tell me – what was in front of me. The money is more than I ever thought I would see in my lifetime."

"So, what is the matter, Kostik?" asked Nikita. "Are you scared to do this?"

Kostik looked at Nikita. He was unhappy being asked if he was scared. It sounded like Nikita was was telling Kostik that he was scared. He was angry but realized he would probably ask the same questions to someone he knew in a similar situation. Yes, he told himself, I am scared.

"Come, Kostik," Nicholas entered the conversation. "You are not a weakling. Look what you have done with yourself over the last ten years. I want to work for someone who knows what he wants and goes after it. I'm sure Nikita feels the same way. Nyet, Nikita? You have reached for some of your dreams and made them real. What you got now is a bigger dream and you are reaching out for it. You will grab it. You will make it come alive, and I thank you for letting me go with you."

"I can't talk as good as Nicholas, Kostik. I feel the same way what he said to you. I am happy we found you, and I am proud to work with someone like you, and I thank you, too, as Nicholas said."

All three were silent. Kostik had difficulty keeping his emotions in check, but not entirely. He could not speak without his voice breaking. Nicholas and Nikita remained silent. They knew what they had said struck Kostik and they both understood, without saying anything to each other. This was not the time to say anything further.

Kostik broke the silence. "You don't know what you have done for me. Yes, I am scared, and I will be scared for some time, but you two gave me a belief in myself I need right now and I won't forget it. I won't let you down. You both thanked me. The thank you should be from me to you, and it is. Thank you." With that, he approached both men, shook hands and hugged each one, burying his face in each one's shoulder. With his eyes teary, he said, "We have work to do." All three laughed.

Kostik contacted Ozkowski who had told him he would start clearing the lot in two weeks because he had to finish a job he started. Kostik, had to bury his disappointment that the job couldn't be started tomorrow and told him what Louizeaux had said. Ozkowski understood.

This little stone wall, as Kostik saw it, gave him time to review his figures concerning what he had to order from the lumber yard he chose. Satisfied with his decision, he drove to the yard to give his first order.

The two weeks dragged by, so thought Kostik. Fortunately, all preparatory work, thanks to Louizeaux, was completed, including buying the property with money given to him by Henry's bank. Ozkowski kept his word; his equipment arrived on the fourteenth day and Kostik was there to greet it with a huge smile. Nicholas and Nikita let out a loud cheer.

Ozkowski heard the yelling and walked to the three. "What's going on?" he asked.

"We are so glad to see you and your equipment," answered Kostik. "Now, we really believe it."

Three weeks after Kostik had ordered the materials, the lumberyard delivered a truckload to the site on which Kostik's first house would be built. He stood on the curb of the lot and just took in the sight of the beginning of the project, and his anticipated future.

CHAPTER THIRTY-FIVE

Watching from just out of earshot was a young man who happened to walk up. After Ozkowski started his bulldozers, the young man walked to Kostik, Nikita and Nicholas. Unable to speak English – or Russian – the man tried with hand signals to indicate his interest. He instinctively tried to speak what he was signaling.

"He is I-talian," said Nicholas and emphasized Italian by pronouncing the I as 'eye'.

"Si," the young man answered.

"Can you understand what he is trying to tell us?" Kostik asked his two men. Both just shrugged their shoulders. "How can we...I think he's trying to tell us he wants to work and that he can maybe do what Bernie is doing."

"I take him over to Bernie," said Kostik. He motioned for the man to come with him. Kostik explained to Bernie what was happening.

"Do this, Kostik. You write a note in big American letters saying you can't talk with the man and whoever reads this note and can speak I-talian could you please write down what he is trying to tell me. I think he might want to work. Make certain you write your name at the bottom of the note. I have done this a couple of times, and it sometimes works," offered Ozkowski.

"I will do it," Kostik said. Kostik wrote the note, gave it to the man and somehow was able to convey what he wanted the man to do. The man smiled, nodded his head, took Kostik's hand and shook it. With that, he rushed away. Several hours later, he returned with a very pretty, young Italian woman.

"I am looking for Kostik," she said in perfect American with no accent.

"I Kostik. Did he show you sign?"

"Yes, he did. He is my cousin. He just arrived from Italy a few days ago. He explained that he saw this work going on and wanted to know what is going on here. Oh, I'm sorry. I didn't introduce myself. I am Angelina Bellini, and he is Vincenzo Bellini, my father's nephew." She put her hand out which Kostik took and shook hands with her.

"What kind work he does?" Kostik asked her.

"Vincenzo, come here," she called in Italian and told him to tell her what he does; what does he know how to do.

After he told her, she asked how he did the work. When he told her, she looked at Kostik and looked back at her cousin. She asked him if he was joking with her. Somewhat miffed, he said no, but then smiled. She turned to Kostik. "He digs cellars."

"All right. Where his equipment is?" Kostik asked.

"He has to buy a plow horse and plow," she answered.

Hesitating, Angelina was skeptical and did not expect Kostik's reaction.

"Do you know how old he is, Angelina? Ask him, also, how many cellars he has done? How long he worked for the person who taught him? Did he leave that person to start on his own? How did he do on his own and why, if he did good, why he came to America?"

"Wait a minute, Kostik. That's a lot of questions, and I'm not sure I remember them all," she laughed.

"Please stay with us if you can and go through all these questions with Vincenzo and pass on his answers to Bernie and me. Is that okay?"

Kostik turned to his carpenters. "She said she would, so I will stay with her and Vincenzo, and we will see what happens. If I hire him, you will be working with him, so why don't you both stay too." Kostik said softly, "I know you want to look on her more than you want to look on Bernie's bulldozer," he laughed. He turned, and noticed Angelina had heard what he had said and was blushing, but not totally in embarrassed.

Vincenzo was twenty-six years old, had successfully worked for and with the person from whom he learned his trade, and went into business for himself at the end of the First World War. He came to America because of the extent of destruction and corruption prevalent where he lived. He believed he would fare better in the United States. Kostik talked with Nicholas and Nikita who agreed with him. With that decision, Kostik went to talk with Ozkowski who also agreed to give the young immigrant a chance.

Kostik returned to Angelina and Vincenzo. When Kostik told Angelina to tell Vincenzo he would hire him and help him get a horse and plow, Angelina screamed (in stereotypical Italian emotion), threw her arms around

Kostik's neck and proceeded to hug and kiss him rather profusely. Vincenzo just stared, not understanding. When Angelina told him, he, too, became emotional, grabbed Kostik's hands, kissed them and then hugged him. All Kostik could say was "My goodness!"

Finally, when all of the emotions were expended, they calmed down. Kostik told Angelina she had to go with him and Vincenzo to interpret in the negotiations for the horse and plow. She agreed.

Nicholas and Nikita looked at each other, grinned and looked at Kostik, still grinning.

"What you are grinning about?" asked Kostik.

"Oh, nothing, Kostik. Nothing," Nicholas answered.

Kostik said something not nice in Russian, but was smiling broadly as he said it.

Ozkowski cleared the land allowing a clearing where Kostik's materials could be neatly stacked and another where Vincenzo could start digging the cellar. The weather was very good which allowed the cellar work to move at a good pace. It didn't take too long for Kostik, Nicholas and Nikita to begin laying out the measurements for the foundation of the house.

Rather than wait until the digging of the cellar was completed, Kostik told the lumberyard what part of his order he wanted delivered and when. As it was delivered, the four men (plus Angelina telling Vincenzo how Kostik wanted it) separated the materials and placed them in construction order.

It did not take long for Kostik to realize he needed a few more workers, not just anybody off the street but skilled laborers who knew how to lay blocks, lay a cement floor and build block walls. Because of his work in Czar Nickolas's construction company, Kostik knew whether the prospective employees possessed the building skills they claimed to have. He was able to find several men and hired them. He sat Nicholas and Nikita down and talked seriously with them. He thought highly of them and after speaking individually with them, he made each one a foreman in charge of various areas of the construction process.

CHAPTER THIRTY-SIX

"Hey, Kostik, I want to ask you something." said Nicholas. "What do you do for fun?"

"For fun?" Kostik answered.

"Yeah, for fun. Do you ever go out? Do you know any girls? What do you do at night?"

"I think about the house – what has to be done next day, what materials I have to order when..." Kostik started answer.

"That's baloney, Kostik. You have to learn to enjoy life a little bit."

"Is that right? What do you suggest I should do?" Kostik asked, smiling.

"Go someplace where you can meet some girls. Do you know how to dance?"

"I can do it Cossack dance," Kostik answered laughing.

"Oh, Kostik, for crying out loud! I'm not being funny now," said Nicholas.

"All right, Nicholas. Are you talking going to bar? Thank you, but no thank you. I went once with roommates. Never again." Kostik then told him what had happened.

"Oh, for Pete's sake, Kostik. You gonna base one time on forever? How 'bout you go with me and Nikita. I promise you we won't let that happen."

"Where, Timoshenko's bar? What if that girl is there? Then what?"

"We won't go to Timoshenko's bar. There are others. How 'bout you ask Ivan to go with us."

"That would be a surprise to Ivan and to Eugenia. I don't go anyplace except to bed when I go to the house, so I could get up early for work."

"What a life, Kostik. What a life! What are you, ninety-five years old?"

"No, hundred ninety-five," Kostik laughed. "All right, I go."

Kostik told Eugenia that he was going out Saturday night with Nicholas and Nikita.

"I would like it if Ivan could go with us. I certainly don't want anything to happen like last time. We are not going to Timoshenko's, so that makes me feel better."

"Kostik, your voice sounds like you are not really looking forward to doing this," Eugenia said.

"Well, I am little bit nervous. I am not used to lots of peoples, noisy places, things like that," answered Kostik.

"You know, Kostik, the boys are right. You need to get out. You can't just sleep and go to work, sleep and go to work. What about your teacher friend? Why you couldn't get a date with her. She's very pretty, and I think she liked you."

"She has boyfriend, and I don't know how to act with a girl."

"Ever since I know you, you never go to church. Do you think you would feel better meeting people in that kind of situation instead of a bar?"

"I don't know, Eugenia. I am not used to both places."

"Well, I think it is time you got used to one over the other," Eugenia spoke sharply.

"I am going to see what happens. Maybe it wouldn't be so bad. We will see."

Eugenia talked with Ivan who agreed to join Kostik, Nicholas and Nikita.

CHAPTER THIRTY-SEVEN

"Well, Kostik, what do you think?" asked Ivan. "Did you have fun? Would you like to go out again?"

"Yeah, I think so. This was much better than last time, but are bars the only the place to go out?"

"Where would you like to go, Kostik?" asked Nicholas.

"I would like to learn more about the United States. What about library or maybe museum or something like that?" asked Kostik. He was serious.

The three men laughed. Kostik was not laughing.

"Why are you laughing?" Kostik said somewhat loudly and hurt.

"I'm sorry, Kostik," answered Ivan. "We are not laughing at you."

"Oh no? What do you call it? Mooing like a cow?" questioned Kostik accusatorily.

"Well, we'll see what we can work out," said Ivan.

Several weeks passed since this little altercation and there was nothing social that was suggested to Kostik that interested him; however, Eugenia approached Kostik with a thought that he said he would think about. St. Adalbert, a Roman Catholic Polish Church in Elizabeth was attended by many young people, more so than attended the Russian Orthodox Church.

"I think it might be good for you to break away from only those young people that work with and for you. I don't say completely, Kostik. Meet other young people. You know what I mean, Kostik?"

"Yes, I do, Eugenia," Kostik answered. "But, I don't know anybody there, and I don't know anybody I could talk to who knows anybody who goes to that church."

"Ask Nicholas and Nikita if they do."

The two of them said they knew people who went to the church, and they would introduce him to them. Kostik had them arrange for them to go to a diner to get acquainted which worked out very well. Within a few weeks, it was decided to take Kostik to the church social.

As generally happens, Kostik was not immediately accepted by the young men. He was quite handsome, though slight of stature, but definitely a threat to the status-quo of the male-female relationships. Kostik was not sure enough of himself to even approach a young woman with whom to talk. He talked with Eugenia, expressing his inability to get up the necessary nerve to even say hello to a girl. He knew, too, that his English was not that terrific which frightened him even more.

Eugenia counseled him wisely, advising him to take his time and assured him that with patience he would be able to approach a young woman. Kostik replied that he was not so sure but that he would not stop going to the Catholic church.

One Sunday after church, a man who looked to be in his twenties came to Kostik. He spoke English.

"Hello, my name is Dominic Kutkowski. I have seen you here for several weeks and noticed nobody talks with you. Do you know why, and what is your name?"

"My name is Kostik Kopituk. I tried to talk with some of the young men, but they won't talk with me," answered Kostik.

Kostik was pleased that someone would finally talk with him. The two had a rather long discussion, asking each other the usual 'get-acquainted questions'. They parted with Dominic telling Kostik he would find out why the others refused to talk to him.

Dominic broke the ice. When he found out why the other men had shunned Kostik, Dominic laughed at them and told them that what they had been doing was absolutely wrong. Apparently, he was a leading member of the group and did not have a problem, both chastising and turning them around. Fortunately for Kostik, this young man recognized the difficulties some immigrants have in meeting people and stepped forward to correct the problem. Kostik learned later that Dominic's grandfather had experienced the same dilemma at this church many years before.

At one of the parties to which Kostik was invited, there was a very pretty girl who attracted Kostik's attention; however, when she returned his glance, he shyly looked away and walked toward one of his new-found male friends.

"Hey, Kostik. I noticed that pretty girl looking at you. I think she probably would like to talk to you, and I saw you looking at her but as soon as she looked at you, you turned and ran. What's the matter with you?" he asked. "She is really good-looking."

"Yes, I know that, but I don't know how to talk, what I should say," said Kostik shrugging his shoulders.

Dominic saw Kostik talking to another man and walked over to speak to them.

"Dominic, there is this girl over there who looks interested in Kostik, and he might be interested in her but he doesn't know how to 'talk to girls' he says."

"I guess I'll have to have a talk with him," said Dominic. "Kostik, come here," he called.

Dominic had Kostik sit down and began telling him the ins and outs of talking with the opposite sex. "It is going to take getting used to, Kostik, and it is going to take practice. What you have to do is stop being afraid to talk..." said Dominic.

"How do you stop being afraid?" asked Kostik.

"That's up to you, Kostik. The easiest thing to do is to do it."

"That tells me not much," laughed Kostik.

It did take some time but eventually Kostik got up his nerve and approached the girl after church one Sunday.

"Good afternoon. My name is Kostik – Kostik Kopituk."

"Hello," she answered without hesitation. "My name is Anna Krawczyk. I am from Scotch Plains and come to St. Adalbert Church in Elizabeth every Sunday. You are not Polish, are you?"

"No," Kostik answered. "I came to America from Russia."

"When did you come?"

"1910."

"And your parents?" she asked because she guessed correctly that Kostik had arrived while he was still young.

"My father is dead, my mother is still in Russia. I came to America by myself."

Anna was shocked. "By...yourself? My goodness! Do you mean it?"

"Yes, I mean it, Anna," Kostik answered smiling at her reaction.

"Tell me how you did it," Anna said. She could not hide the astonishment in her voice as she rushed out to touch his forearm which surprised Kostik.

"Anna," her mother called out to her from across the room. "Are you ready to go?" She didn't wait for an answer, turned and with Anna's father walked toward the door. Anna stood, told Kostik she had to go and asked if he would be coming to church next week to which he answered that he would. He stood and watched her leave the room – with a big smile on his face.

"Well, I see you broke the ice," Dominic said with his own big smile.

"I what? What ice did I break?" answered Kostik.

Dominic chuckled. "No, Kostik. That's just a saying. All it means is....."

"I think I know what it means – I finally learned how to talk to a girl," Kostik said laughing, "but her mother and father made her leave."

"Well, you know what you have to do next week," Dominic said as he put his hand on Kostik's shoulder.

"Yeah, I know." Almost instantly Kostik said. "No, I don't know. What I am doing next week?"

"You're going to ask Anna to go out with you," answered Dominic.

Kostik was completely taken aback. "You're crazy, Dominic. I can't ask her to go out with me."

"And why can't you?"

Kostik was trying to come up with excuses as to why he could not. Every one he offered, Dominic countered with why Kostik could.

"I'll tell you what, Kostik. If you'll feel better, I'll call my girlfriend, and we'll go with you and Anna.

"You will? That would be wonderful. Oh, yes, that would be very nice." Kostik said almost ecstatically.

"But wait, Kostik. I think you should take the opportunity to meet her parents at church before you ask her to go out. It's always good to let the parents see who it is their daughter is going out with. Of course, you're not going to ask her out in front of her mother and father or even at church this time. Another time might be okay, but not this time. It will be best if you call on the telephone."

Dominic then told Kostik what he should say if her father answers the phone, what to say if her mother answers the phone.

The first date went very well, and the dating continued, blossoming into a courtship. During this period, Kostik sold the first house he built. When all the necessary documentation had been completed, Kostik and Mr. Louizeaux prepared the next steps for the additional houses Kostik wanted to construct.

CHAPTER THIRTY-EIGHT

Louizeaux contacted the owner of the land who had agreed to sell it to Kostik. All the necessary preparations were completed. The city was involved and approved all the plans: roadwork, water, sewers, sewer tap-ins for each house, etc. Henry's bank approved all the monies Kostik would need to order his building materials. Kostik was on his way – again – hiring work crews, various contractors (the numbers having to be expanded) and attorneys to see that every 't' was crossed, every 'i' was dotted. The block-long-plus project was now in definite motion. Kostik hoped that Anna felt as he did, that the two of them should get married. He thought her parents would be receptive, but he really was not sure – particularly her mother. She was a tough one.

Kostik was Russian Orthodox, not Roman Catholic. In discussions about religion, Anna had indicated that her mother was afraid of the priests and nuns and the control they had over the Polish people.

Kostik decided it might be a good idea to talk with the pastor at the church. He asked Dominic for the priest's name. When Dominic asked why, Kostik told him but said he should keep it a secret until he could talk with Anna's parents after he spoke with the priest. Dominic told Kostik that it would be very good for him to talk to Father Masnicki, the priest. "Kostik, let me warn you, he is going to try to change your mind. If you are serious about this, you are going to have to stand strong, not back down. But – and I have seen you when you get irritated – don't lose your temper. Just stay calm. He has his requirements to follow. Understand that. A Russian Orthodox man marrying a Catholic girl could create a problem for the priest," Dominic said with a chuckle. "It's not the nationalities. It's the religion problem."

CHAPTER THIRTY-NINE

Kostik thanked Dominic and left to go to the church to make an appointment with Father Masnicki.

"Ah, Kostik, come in. What can I do for you?" the priest asked.

"Father, I need to talk to you 'bout something very serious and secret now. Are you allowed to keep a secret?"

"Yes, of course. I've had to do just that many times. What is your secret?"

"I want to marry Anna Krawczyk but I have not told anyone except Dominic Kutkowski who has become a friend at church. He will not tell anyone. He knows I am talking to you; in fact, he said I should." This pleased Father Masnicki.

Dominic was right – the priest did not like the idea of Kostik marrying Anna.

"Why you don't like me to marry Anna? I love her, she loves me. We enjoy each other..."

"She told you she does? She said that?"

"Yes," answered Kostik.

"Remember, she's just a young kid. This is new excitement for her," said the priest.

"You think she doesn't mean it?"

"For right now, she does. Remember, this is exciting. She can tell her friends and her relatives who will all be happy for her."

The bantering went back and forth for quite some time, friendly and angry at times. When the bantering ended, the priest's voice was uncompromising.

"Kostik, let me enumerate for you all the things wrong with this. First...."

"What is that word you said?" Kostik asked.

"See, Kostik? There's number one: you don't even know American words. Anna has an education. You do not. Your culture is different from hers. Your language is different from hers."

"What are you talking about Father? We both talk American."

It was beginning to get nasty. Kostik tried to keep calm, but he was having difficulty doing so. The priest began talking down to Kostik, using big words he did not yet understand.

"I'll tell you what, Kostik. If you agree to become Catholic, I will do what is necessary to convince Anna's parents to let you marry her."

Kostik felt he was being trapped which he did not like. He remembered what Anna had told him about how her mother was controlled. He vowed to himself that he would not let that happen to himself and certainly not to Anna. However, when he was asked later, all he said was that everything was okay, even to Dominic.

CHAPTER FORTY

Kostik left the church and drove to Scotch Plains to talk with Anna's mother and father. If they agreed, he would immediately ask her to marry him right then and there.

When he arrived at the house, Kostik's knees began shaking. He was not used to this kind of situation. He tried to stop his shaking, so he could stand straight and not fall down – which he felt like doing. He thought if he knocked on the door soft enough, they would not answer the door, so he could come back later – or tomorrow. Her father answered the door.

"Hello, Kostik. Come in. Anna is out with the dog somewhere. Come in," he said again. "Is something wrong?" he asked, recognizing something was wrong with Kostik.

"Is Anna's mother home?" Kostik asked. "If she is, could she come here?"

She heard Kostik and Anthony, Anna's father, talking and entered the room. Before anything more was said, Kostik told them he wanted to talk with them without Anna.

"I would like to tell...." Kostik started, fidgeting from the left foot, then the right. "I want to..." he coughed, "ask you if you...will let...me ask...Anna," he cleared his throat," to...marry me." Silence! Anthony swore in Polish, smiling. Anna's mother, Catherine, started to cry. Looking stunned, they both just looked at each other.

The usual parental questions followed, one right after another in rapid fire. Kostik tried to step in several times and when he finally got an opening, he asked if they approved of the marriage. Both answered 'yes' together and then asked if he had asked Anna.

"No, I did not, but if it's all right, I'll wait for her to come back and ask then," he answered.

"I hope her answer will be the one I want to hear."

"The way she has been..." Catherine started.

"Stop, Catherine," Anthony said loudly.

CHAPTER FORTY-ONE

"Stop what?" asked Anna as she came through the door. "Kostik, what are you doing here?" she asked smiling broadly as she turned to face him. Catherine and Anthony hastily left the couple to themselves.

"What is happening?" Anna asked as Kostik stepped toward her.

"I have a question I need to ask you," he said, taking her hands in his.

"Kostik, what..."

"Anna, will you...." He cleared his throat which he had promised himself he would not do.

"Anna, will...you," he coughed, "will...you...marry...me?" He blurted 'me' before he had a chance to again cough or clear his throat.

"Kostchick..." seriously taken by complete surprise. "Kostchick," she used a term of endearment for Kostik for the first time.

"Anna?" he questioned again.

"Kostchick. Yes! Yes!" Anna pressed herself against Kostik, buried her face in his neck and shoulder. "Yes!" again. Her parents had heard it all, rushed into the room and put their arms around them.

Now, Kostik had to take Anna to buy the engagement ring. He wanted her to pick it out.

CHAPTER FORTY-TWO

Two weeks after Anna and Kostik's engagement party, Reverend Masnicki called Anna to tell her it was necessary for both Kostik and her to meet with him in his office at St. Adalbert Church.

"What is this for, Father?" Anna asked.

"It is customary for the marrying couple to meet with the pastor of the church to discuss certain matters of importance concerning the marriage. I would like to meet with the two of you next Saturday. Will you contact Kostik and tell him about this. Ask him if ten in the morning is acceptable. Please tell me by tomorrow so I can make arrangements. I will expect your call. Thank you, Anna. Goodbye."

On Saturday morning, Kostik picked Anna up in Scotch Plains. Kostik asked Anna if she knew the reason for the meeting. She told him what little she knew and laughed, saying they would both find out together.

"I want you to both know how important this meeting is. It is to make certain you both know the importance of establishing a Catholic marriage and Catholic home. Now, Kostik, you are Russian Orthodox, is that correct?" Reverend Masnicki said to the couple. "I have papers I need you to sign, Kostik stating that you and Anna will raise your children in the Catholic faith." He continued to emphasize the work 'Catholic.'

"We do not have children, Father," said Kostik.

"No, but when you do have children, you <u>must</u> raise them in the <u>Catholic</u> faith," answered the priest, emphasizing the words 'must' and Catholic.

I can't sign that now. When the time comes, we will talk about it. What do you say, Anna?" said Kostik.

"What happens if Kostik doesn't sign the paper now?" Anna asked.

"Well, we can't marry you in the Sanctuary. I would have to marry you in the Sacristy,"

Reverend Masnicki answered with a stern tone to his voice, "and Anna's mother will <u>not</u> accept that, I will tell you." He said even stronger and more harshly, "You will have to sign the paper, Kopituk, whether you like it or not!"

"I'll talk to my mother," Anna entered the conversation. She recognized the priest was becoming angry, and she knew he did not like his authority to be challenged.

"Remember, Kostik, I cannot marry you in the Sanctuary. What will you do to satisfy Anna's mother?" the priest asked again.

"It will be all right. I will build a church in the living room of the house. I will build an altar, church benches, hang a Crucifix on the wall, call my Russian priest to marry us, and it will be beautiful," said Kostik in as bright and cheery tone as possible. He did not like Rev. Masnicki. With that, Anna and Kostik left the church.

CHAPTER FORTY-THREE

When Anna told her mother of the situation, she was immediately unnerved and took her daughter into another room and closed the door. Since she was a very strong-willed woman, she laid down the law with Anna, demanding that Anna make Kostik sign the papers or else.

"How will you know you are really married?" Anna's mother asked. "Didn't you say Father Masnicki said he would not be able to marry you in the actual church? If you are not married in the actual church, then you will not be considered married. You will be living in sin. You have to find a different man."

Anna started to cry. She was always brow-beaten by her mother; she rarely come out on top in an argument with her. She ran from the room and out of the house onto the front porch. When her mother followed, Anna continued to run into the yard and out into the field. Her father saw her and caught her.

When Anna told her father what had happened, the normally mild-mannered man became angry and put his arms around his young, more favored daughter. He took her hand and because of her state of mind, Anna stubbornly refused to go toward the house with him. As he started to pull her, she strongly resisted until her father calmed her. When they returned to the house, he told her to wait on the porch because her mother had gone back into the house.

Her father, in a very unusual demeaner for him, began to berate Anna's mother. A very strong argument ensued. Anna's mother was shocked at the tone of voice of her husband, a tone she had rarely – almost never – heard before. It frightened her. Anna's father was quite surprised when he realized had taken command of the situation and continued to assert himself. When Anna's mother said she could no longer live in the house, her father stood virtually nose-to-nose with her until she backed away. He told her in no uncertain terms that she was not going throw Anna out of the house.

"What are you and Kostik planning to do, Anna?" her father asked.

"Have our wedding in this house." Anna answered on the verge of tears. "Kostik said he would make an altar and benches like our church benches for our living room and make it look like a church."

"What kind of crazy thing is that going to be?" Anna's mother interjected loudly. "Who is going to be the priest?"

"Kostik said he would call his priest, Mama."

"Anna, you will not be married! You know Father Masnicki will not approve," her mother yelled. "We are Catholic, not Russian Orthodox!"

"Are you saying all the people who marry in the Russian church are not married?" Anna answered.

"No, of course not. I'm not saying that. Don't be a smart-alec!"

"What are you saying then?"

"I am not saying anything."

So ended the argument.

Shortly after supper, Kostik came into the house. Anna met him in the living room.

"Anna, what did you mother and father say about what I want to do?"

"Oh, Kostik, I don't know. Maybe you should talk to my father."

"Are they against the idea?"

"No, my mother is. She said we wouldn't be married if we don't marry in the church

"Oh, for cryin' out loud. I never heard of such a thing. That's crazy! My mother and father were not married? My sister and brother-in-law are not married?" Kostik said angrily. "Where is your father?"

"I think in the backyard," answered Anna.

Kostik found Anna's father. "Anthony," – Kostik called him by his first name – "what do you think of my plan?"

"It's not what I think, Kostik. It's Anna's mother. You have to make her agree."

"Don't you have anything to say, Anthony?"

"This is very big, Kostik."

"Big or no big, do you like it?"

"Yes, but..."

"No 'buts', Anthony. You like it, Anna likes it, you both know my work, and I like it. Let us all three sit down with her."

"We could do that but you are going to have to convince her that we all are not going to be kicked out of the church by Father Masnicki, not just this church, Kostik, but the whole Catholic church."

"Anthony, Masnicki is not your Pope. He can't do that. He is just a priest. Think what you are saying."

"I'm not saying it – Anna's mother is."

"I will call Masnicki and ask him," Kostik said laughing.

"Daddy, this is not funny," said Anna who overheard Anthony and Kostik as she started to cry.

"Everything will be all right, Anna," Kostik said as he put his arm around her shoulders and wiped the tears from her cheeks. "Better yet, I will go to see him tomorrow morning when I go to work. I will get it taken care of, Anna. Don't worry."

Kostik drove by the work site, checked the one house that was near completion and drove away satisfied. He drove to St. Adalbert Church.

Kostik was not sure what he was going to say to the priest nor how he was going to say it.

He parked his truck and walked into the church to Reverend Masnicki's office. The priest was in.

"Good morning, Masnicki (no mention of Father, Reverend or anything else). I need to speak to you," said Kostik.

"Hello, Kostik. What can I do for you?"

"You can convince Anna's mother that because Anna will not be married in this church and that my Russian priest will be doing what you would usually be doing, Anna's whole family will not be – how you call it – kicked out of the church – the whole Catholic church; and, also, Anna and me will be, will yes, be married."

"Anna's mother believes that and that you won't be married?" Masnicki asked astonished. "Who is going to kick them out of the Catholic faith?"

"You."

"Me?! I can't do that. I don't have the power to excommunicate them. That's the word for 'kicking them out of the church', Kostik," the priest answered.

"I knew it was a big word, but I didn't remember it," Kostik chuckled. "Will you call Anna's mother."

"Tell me Kostik, have you arranged for your priest yet?"

"No, I haven't called him yet."

Reverend Masnicki kept asking questions about the Russian priest, suggesting since time is getting short, he may have other plans.

Kostik stopped Masnicki. "Are you hinting Masnicki? Do you want to do the wedding? Stop beating the bush or however you say that saying."

"You are doing it in Anna's house, no?"

"Yes."

Again, Masnicki went off on a tangent.

"Masnicki, stop! I will pay you. How much do you want?" Kostik said, somewhat miffed.

"Yes, Kostik, I would very much like to do the wedding for you. Is it still September twenty-eighth?"

"That's correct. We haven't decided on the time. I will call you and let you know. How much do you want?" Kostik asked again, a bit harshly because of having to ask again and again.

"My goodness, Kostik, you make it sound so serious about how much."

"So, tell me, Masnicki."

"You know I don't have a car. Can you pick me up and take me back?"

"I could do that. What about paying you?" Kostik asked again.

"Well, I normally charge..."

"Just tell me how much." Kostik was becoming angry.

"Fifteen dollars," Reverend Masnicki answered, somewhat angered by being talked to like Kostik was doing.

"All right, that's fine. I will pay you twenty dollars," Kostik said with a smile which made the priest smile. "Now I want you to call Anna's mother, tell her she will still be a Catholic and Anna and Kostik will be married. Can you call right now?"

Reverend Masnicki made the call and was able to calm Anna's mother's fears. Kostik shook hands with the priest, left the church and drove to the construction site.

CHAPTER FORTY-FOUR

Kostik waited until lunchtime and called Nikita and Nicholas to have lunch with him.

"I have a job for you both. It has nothing to do with these houses. It's going to have to be done after work and on Saturday and Sunday if you will do it."

He explained what he wanted to do with the living room at Anna's house.

"Are you serious, Kostik? You want to build a room in Anna's house to look like a church with an altar, benches and everything else the priest might need like tables and chairs. Are you crazy?"

"I guess so but, it has to be done," Kostik said laughing. He then explained why.

"Okay, Kostik. When do you want to start?"

They got together that evening after work and made all the measurements they would need. The next day Kostik ordered all the material to be delivered and escorted the delivery truck to Scotch Plains. He directed how he wanted the material to be laid out. Kostik and his two foremen began work on the project the next evening. They soon learned they would need several more carpenters if the "church" were to be built in time.

"Hey, Kostik," called Nikita. "About your wedding...I know you are going fast, but I thought you might have forgotten something. No, I don't want the job, but have you thought of who you are going to have for a 'best man'?"

"Oh my gosh, no; but, I know exactly who – Henry Louizeaux."

Kostik knew this was more important than just a phone call, therefore he drove to the bank the next day. Henry was very pleased, thanked and hugged Kostik, but suggested that it might be better to have one of Kostik's countrymen stand with him. He suggested Ivan Petrovich, who was very surprised and said no when asked.

"Why not you, Ivan?" Kostik asked. "You were the first Russian man I met after I got from the boat and who has watched over me like a big brother, protected me from wild, wild women and gave me very good advice to keep me straight. Please, do this Ivan," Kostik said as he put both hands on Ivan's shoulders.

Eugenia Nevar was with Kostik when he asked Ivan. "You cannot say no, Ivan. You have been a very important part of Kostik's life for fourteen years, and this is a way for him to show you how important you are to him. He accepts, Kostik," Eugenia answered for Ivan. The three had a good laugh.

"Remember, Kostik, I do not speak American," said Ivan. "If I have to talk, what......"

"Oh my, that's right," said Kostik. "Let me think a minute."

"Kostik, what about Anna Polikov? Do you think she could say in American what Ivan is saying?" Eugenia asked.

"You mean – what is it called? You mean change what he is saying in Russian into American? I will call her to see if she can – and will do it," said Kostik.

Kostik and Ivan drove to Anna's house that evening, explained what was needed and after serious pleading – and begging – she agreed to try, but she wanted to practice with Ivan.

Ivan and Anna practiced several evenings with Ivan saying a few sentences in Russian followed by Anna's English translation. After several tries they became familiar with the process.

The 'living room-to-church' conversion project was completed on time. The invited guests marveled at the transformation of the room. Both of Anna's parents were pleased with the outcome.

Both Father Masnicki and the priest from the Russian Orthodox Church, officiated at the wedding each performing a part of the service as they combined the two religions. The newlyweds received many compliments from the guests and especially from Anna's mother. Anna and Kostik were so happy with the results.

Although the wedding was small the reception featured an abundance of Polish and Russian food. Most of the foods were actually quite similar, differing only in their ethnic names, and most attendees had little trouble recognizing what they were eating.

CHAPTER FORTY-FIVE

Ivan and Anna Polikov rose from the table. He picked up a knife and glass and "rang" the glass to begin the dual presentation of the "toast". Ivan began with Anna translating what he had said.

"I would like to introduce to you Kostik and Anna Kopituk, Mr. and Mrs. Kostik Kopituk. It is my honor to introduce to the world for the first time the two of you in your new role as husband and wife. All married roads have bumps. May yours be few and very small, smooth ones. May your lives be long, loving and successful. I know I speak for everyone in this room. We thank you for having us in your circle of friends. To Anna and Kostik." The glasses rose in salute as the people applauded.

"One thing I almost forgot," said Ivan. "I don't know how many of you know how these two met. At the time, Kostik was doing home repairs and additions, including fences. He had just completed the fence in the front of a certain house. This fence had a swinging gate that a small, nine-year-old girl could swing on back and forth. The fence – along with the gate – had a very new, white, wet paint job that could easily have been scratched by a nine-year-old girl with leather-soled shoes swinging on the gate.

Coming from the back of the house, Kostik saw what he did not want to see. A small, - well, you know. He yelled at her as he was running toward her, reached in his belt and threw the hammer he was carrying at her and continued to holler at her to get off the gate. She did and ran very fast from the yard, screaming and crying.

"How strange things sometimes turn out. Here we are ten years later, standing together, celebrating the beginning of what looks like a beautiful new life – with no hammers in sight." The people laughed, applauded Ivan and Anna Polikov while Kostik and Anna laughed and hugged each other.

Soon, as with any wedding, it was time for the bride and groom to begin their life together with a honeymoon. They left that evening for the Catskill Mountains in New York.

CHAPTER FORTY-SIX

Kostik sat down in the kitchen with Anna to discuss the houses he was building. They continued to sell well.

"Anna, almost as quick as we finish one, it gets sold. That makes me feel real good."

"I am proud of you, Kostik. You should be proud, too," Anna said, smiling.

"I never would have dreamed that something like this would be happening to this Russian immigrant. If I stayed in Russia, I would be a peasant working in the Czar's construction company with little chance of improving myself. But here in America, opportunity is available for anybody willing to work hard unlike in Russia where the government determined everything. In Russia, the people are captives. Maybe the walls and the fences are missing but the guards are there. The Revolution did nothing to free the people. All they did was transfer power from one type of government to another. The government people still controls everything unlike here. Too bad the people didn't go far enough. All they did was go from one power to another kind of power. Still – government controls everything – not like here, and I hope I never live to see the day when government controls our lives. If ever the government tries to step on us people, I hope we have the backbone to step back on top of the government. I'm afraid, though, if the government starts to give away so much that people begin to make themselves believe the government is going to take care of them, the government will pay them to sit home and do nothing, then the people become prisoners."

"My goodness, Kostik," said Anna. "I would never have thought about what you have said. I guess, from what you have told me about Russia and your escape, you certainly are lucky you were able to escape. I am so proud of you for what you have done with yourself since you came here," she said as she got up, walked around the table, put her arms around him and kissed him. "I feel so lucky that I married you."

Kostik laughed, "You really think so? I hope so," he said. "Do your mother and father feel that you got the right man?"

"Oh, Kostchick (Anna said using the endearment of Kostik). Now stop that. You should know by now that they do," Anna said as she shook her finger at him.

"Yeah, I'm beginning to think your mother is changing her mind from what she first thought," Kostik answered her. "I wasn't so sure when we started going together. She isn't the easiest person to get close to."

"I know Kostchick. Maybe when the baby comes she will be nicer. When she sees how wonderful a father you're going to be with her grandchild..."

"How do you know what kind of father I am going to be? I might be mean and nasty and yell at the kid all the time."

"Oh, stop Kostchick. You won't be like that. I know you," Again, she got up from the table and hugged him. They both laughed.

"It won't be long. Couple of weeks? We better get the room ready, no? I been thinking about the room color. What do you think of this? We don't know if it's a boy or girl. So, we won't be wrong, how about paint the walls pink and blue stripes? You think your mother would like that?" Kostik knew Anna's reaction.

"Are you crazy, Kostchick? You can't mean it!"

"Of course," he answered.

"Of course what? You mean it? You don't?"

"Yes," Kostik answered playfully.

"Will you stop that! I'm going to hit you!" Anna laughed.

"We got to do the room but, Anna, I want us to start to think about building our own house. I will look for a piece of property. I like Roselle, so I will look there. Do you know Roselle?"

"I'll leave that up to you, Kostchick."

CHAPTER FORTY-SEVEN

The year is 1925, fifteen years since Kostik a sixteen-year-old peasant with a fourth grade education, landed at Ellis Island by himself. He had no parents, no siblings, no relatives of any kind but he was now in the country called America, the country he was told offered opportunity not offered in the "old" country (as it is even today). Fortunately, when he left Ellis Island he came to a Russian-settled community where he met good people and found a job. Of his own volition and with permission from the owner of the company that employed him, he worked to have time off and he took ten-percent of his pay to hire a teacher to teach him English. There were no free programs to teach immigrants English. America made opportunity available; the immigrant had to avail himself of the opportunity and make it work for him. He learned carpentry, construction and remodeling. He was very fortunate that a banker seemed to recognize something in Kostik to make him want to help this young immigrant succeed in America and make a better life for himself. With the banker's help, he bought property on which to construct a house and entered into a purchase contract to buy more if he were successful. He was. True to himself and his station in life, he put many immigrants to work. Now he was about to experience his most wonderful achievement, the birth of his first child.

On June 15, 1925, a son was born to Anna and Kostik Kopituk. They named him after Kostik but used the Anglicized name: Konstantine. It didn't last long. Nurses began calling the baby Connie which was perfectly acceptable – except to Anna.

"Kostchick, we have to change the baby's name," Anna said.

"Change his name? Why for?" Kostik asked startled.

"Because nurses have started calling him Connie and that sounds like a girl's name."

"For cryin' out loud, Anna, I..."

"No, I mean it, Kostik. I don't want my son to have a girl's nickname," Anna stated, folding her arms defiantly (the mood had changed; it is now Kostik, not Kostchick).

"Ann..." Kostik tried to say something.

"Don't Ann me, Kostik! I said I mean it! I'll tell you what: Konstantine can be his middle name."

"That's very nice. What's going in Konstantine's place....Herman, Vasily, Stashek?"

"No, I want something American like maybe (she paused) Raymond."

"Raymond?!" Kostik said loudly. "Where did that name come from?"

"Well, doesn't it sound good? What's the matter with 'Raymond'?"

"It sure doesn't sound Russian or Polish."

"No, it sounds American, Kostchick. Isn't that what we want?"

"Yeah, it is. Raymond Konstantine. It sounds good, Anna. You like it?"

"Thank you, my husband, and thank you, your son's father." With that, Anna hugged Kostik.

"We have to go to the hospital and change the papers."

"Anna, let's go to Roselle when we're finished at the hospital. Like I said, it's time we really started building a house of our own."

"Why don't we look in Elizabeth and Linden, and what's wrong with Scotch Plains?"

It certainly wasn't settled quickly but after a year of looking, they decided on a piece of land in Roselle.

CHAPTER FORTY-EIGHT

Since Kostik was building a rather large development, he had to take a great deal of time to oversee. Despite his oversight, there were snags.

One man who claimed to be a builder (he knew everything about building a house he said) was assigned by Kostik to cut and install that part on which the window sash sits when it is closed. Unfortunately, this man measured the first one he was to cut and install but cut the rest, dozens of others, by eye. In addition, he didn't cut them in the same direction; actually, he cut them upside down. Kostik paid him for his time less a certain amount for the wasted lumber and told him to leave and never come back. The man attacked Kostik. Kostik was faster and although the man was bigger, Kostik quickly subdued him. Several other workers grabbed the man, bodily removed him from the property and rather unceremoniously deposited him in the street. Kostik then picked up the necessary tools and proceeded to cut the lumber correctly.

While the building of Kostik's project continued, he met with Henry Louizeaux to discuss financing his and Anna's house in Roselle and the purchase of the land on which the house was to sit.

"Kostik, young man, I cannot tell you how proud I am of you, what you accomplished and the man you have turned out to be. I would be more than proud to be able to call you my son. I wish I could meet your mother, brothers and sister. What a story I could tell them about you."

Kostik's face turned red with embarrassment and tears filled his eyes. Henry came around from behind the desk to hug Kostik.

"Kostik, all the people at my bank have told me they are happy to have met you. Several have mentioned how happy they are that you feel that America is the greatest country on Earth, as many have heard you say."

"Mr. Louizeaux, America is, and I mean it. I am so lucky to have come here. I'm sure the old country would not have gave me anywhere near what America has gave to me."

Both men were silent for some time as they looked at the floor and out of the window. Both men had to regain their composure.

Henry spoke first. "Now, Kostik." He then cleared his throat. "You want to build your own house."

"Yes, sir. I think it is time we give Anna's mother and father their house back." Kostik said laughing.

"Have you decided where you want to build?" Henry asked. "I mean what town?"

"I found a lot in Roselle that will be perfect. It is just up the street from Warinanko Park. When Raymond gets a little older, he will enjoy playing there. The park is brand new. In fact, it's not completely finished but most was completed in 1923. It even has a lake."

"Let's go see," Henry said.

Henry thought Kostik's choice was good. He had no problems lending him the money to buy the lot and the materials to build the house. When it was finished, the house would be beautiful. It had a fully insulated walk-in attic for storage, three bedrooms and full bath upstairs. On the first floor was a living room, a full-size dining room, kitchen, pantry, office for Kostik, half-bath, entrance to cellar stairs and a screened-in back porch. The basement held the coal-fired furnace which provided the steam to heat the radiators throughout the house, a big room to hold the coal from floor to ceiling, a large playroom with a raised wooden floor and paneled walls, two big washtubs and an open catch-all area on the concrete floor. In back of the house, Kostik built a two-car garage with a huge stand-up attic, a big sandbox for Raymond and an area with a clothesline for Anna to hang the wet household laundry on Mondays. It was a very common sight in that part of the twentieth century to see laundry hanging to dry in all seasons from virtually every household's backyard "clothes line."

CHAPTER FORTY-NINE

"Anna, we are really, finally getting ourselves set by building our own home. But there is also another very important thing I must do. I don't know how long it will take and what I got to do."

"What are you taking about Kostchick?"

"I am talking about it is time I become a true American, an American citizen. As I told Mr. Louizeaux, I thank God for bringing me to the greatest country in the world. I want to say official – is that the right word? – I am an American. I have met too many people from the other side who do not think about becoming American. Some don't even want to talk American. So why did they come here? They should go back where they came from and shut up!"

"Kostchick, calm down," Anna broke in laughing.

"It just makes me so mad, Anna. I tell them to their face to go back. They don't like to be told, but I don't care. They need to be told!"

"I know, Kostchick, I know. You have told workers to pack up their tools and don't come back when you hear them talk bad about America."

"America gives the opportunity. You just need to take it."

"I know, Kostchick. I have heard you many times," said Anna, still chuckling.

"And I will always say it, Anna," said Kostik with strong emphasis.

"Kostchick, go find out about citizenship," Anna said hoping to get Kostik to call Mr. Louizeaux to find out what to do.

"All right, Anna. I will call him," he said as he walked to her and hugged her. He then called Mr. Louizeaux who told him he had to call the county clerk in Elizabeth and follow her instructions.

On January 29, 1926, Kostik submitted the required paperwork to become a United States citizen. On Monday April 5, 1926, the day after

Easter, Kostik received a letter telling him that his application to become a citizen of the United States of America had been accepted and that he needed to come to Elizabeth on April 29, 1926.

On Thursday, April 29, 1926, Kostik arrived at the courthouse in Elizabeth with his young wife, their ten-month-old son and an entourage of virtually everyone who had meant anything to him since he had stepped on American soil in 1910. Things had gone well for Kostik.

The next day, at the site of his big project, his workers cheered when he held up his citizenship papers. When they asked for him to say something, with a trembling voice and tears rolling down his cheeks, he said, "Yesterday was one of the proudest days of my life. I can now say, for true, I, Kostik Kopituk, am an American, a citizen of the United States of America." With that, Kostik broke down. Everyone understood.

Things had gone well for Kostik. He was proud of what he had been able to accomplish and was always quick to state that there had been quite a number of individuals who had given him good advice along the way. One of his proudest moments along with the completion of his big project was the day he became an American citizen. At the completion of the ceremony, Kostik dropped to his knees and thanked God for America and for making himself an American citizen, or as he put it, "a full partner with America."

He was not ashamed nor afraid to say that America had opened the world for him and for many, many immigrants from all over the world.

"America has been basically one thing, an opportunity. As long as I didn't let the government give me anything I didn't work for, I was free to make my life and my family's life. I see what happened to the family I left behind in Russia, and I see what America gave me. The two cannot be compared."

How prophetic of Kostik. America, with the rest of the world, was struck by a global depression. People in America lost homes, businesses, buildings, investments, livelihoods. Fortunately, Kostik had been very frugal with his money. The remodeling and building of houses came to a standstill. The lumber yard that had supplied Kostik was hit very hard and declared bankruptcy. On hearing this, Kostik approached the owner who agreed to sell the business to him; Kostik had the cash with which to do it. Of course, he discussed the idea with Henry Louizeaux who raised concerns, all of which Kostik brazenly countered.

"Kostik, be careful. Don't let your recent success go to your head. This is not a good time. What makes you think you can do better than the present owners who have been in the lumber business for years?"

"Building is still alive at the shore. I believe I can do good down there," Kostik answered and went on to talk very seriously with Henry who could not talk him out of the venture.

Kostik bought the lumber yard and immediately drove to Asbury Park, a city where construction was going on. He learned that many builders thought materials would soon be difficult to acquire. With so much construction going on, a decrease in materials could halt much of the construction. Since Kostik had materials available, one of the owners placed a large order with him.

Several days after receiving the order, Kostik had his huge Mack delivery truck loaded and told the driver where to go. After his truck left, Kostik realized what could happen when the truck arrived to unload. The area had had several days of severe rain that softened the ground into which a heavy truck could easily sink. He immediately ran home, picked up Anna and Raymond and raced after the truck in his new 1930 Model A Ford pickup truck. Although the day was clear and sunny, the favorable weather was not enough to dry out the ground. When they arrived late in the afternoon, the driver was just beginning to back into the area where the materials would be unloaded. Kostik blew his truck's horn and blinked the headlights until his driver stopped backing up.

CHAPTER FIFTY

As Kostik pulled alongside the Mack, the owner of the job site came to tell the driver to continue backing. Kostik waved his hand to his driver indicating to stop.

"Why are you stopping the truck? Back it in to the unloading place," the owner demanded.

"No," answered Kostik. "The ground is too soft for this heavy truck. It will sink."

"You're crazy! Drive it in, I said."

"Wait just a moment," Kostik answered as he went back to his truck. He came back in a few minutes with a sheet of paper on which he had written a statement saying the owner would be responsible for any damages to the land, the Mack – including, but not limited to – its wheels, tires, engine, chassis and damages to the city sidewalk and damage to anything else not foreseen if and when the Mack might need to be towed, plus the cost of the wrecker trucks for towing and any damage to them. "Now, you sign this paper, and we'll then back the truck."

"Gimme the paper. I'll sign, and I will never hire you again."

"Please," Kostik said after he took back the signed paper witnessed by two of the owner's men, "all of these men standing around need work. Hire them to unload the truck."

"That's the dumbest thing you could have said, Kopituk. Just back the truck."

"Okay," Kostik answered as he turned to tell his driver to back the truck.

The driver started the Mack and began backing slowly. It rolled one truck length and at another half a truck length, the sidewalk cracked and the truck broke through and settled into the sand.

"Give it the gas. It will make it," the owner yelled.

The wheels spun and dug the Mack deeper. It now could not move back nor forward. It had dug itself down, axle deep.

Dusk was beginning and several more men than were originally hired began rushing to get it unloaded.

"Well, Kopituk, you were right. Now we're going to have to get a tow truck," the owner said in a very dejected voice.

"I think you're going to need two tow trucks," Kostik answered. "Call one and he will tell us if he is going to need a second one."

The first truck came, attached a chain and began pulling as the Mack driver applied a small amount of gas. The chain broke, smashed the Mack's radiator, hood and windshield.

The owner let out a stream of profanity. He told the tow truck driver to call another tow truck and at Kostik's suggestion, told him to get another to stand by just in case. The two tow trucks sat next to each other and three chains from each tow truck were attached resulting in six chains attached to the Mack. As the pulling began, darkness started to set in. The Mack's wheels began to dig in and some forward motion could be seen. Shortly after forward motion was seen, a major portion of Asbury Park went black. The Mack's wheels had cut through the underground cable. Lights went out in many sections of the city. Immediately, police sirens began to sound; kerosene lanterns appeared out of nowhere; fire trucks pulled out and parked in their respective outside driveways, ready to run as needed. In a few short minutes, police cars showed up at the damaged site.

Kostik told the police what had happened. He explained everything from the arrival of the Mack to its current position still axle deep in the sand. The police contacted the electric company that very quickly sent technicians and supervisors to the site. The major discussion centered on how to remove the Mack. They decided it had to be removed from the hole it had inadvertently been dug into. The electric company's engineers devised the plan to remove the Mack. Several hours after the necessary equipment together, was assembled, the Mack was finally pulled out of the trench.

Kostik stayed with the Mack. Since the removal had taken so long, the police found a comfortable place where Anna and Raymond could wait.

Kostik met with the owner once his Mack was out. "I'm sorry this all happened to you," he said.

"I'm sorry, too, Kopituk."

"Sometimes it is good to listen to someone who has knowledge about something you have none," Kostik answered as he turned to leave.

"Kopituk," the owner called. "I will be ordering from you."

CHAPTER FIFTY-ONE

Kostik kept the yard for four years and sold it in 1933. With the money, he had received from the sale, he bought a Buick, a make of car he had wanted for years. In the same year he resumed remodeling and building houses; he decided not to undertake any more multi-house projects. His reputation to which he gave little thought had been growing for years. His word, handshake and his integrity served him well. He did not lack for customers (his last customer – in this instance, nonpaying, of course – was his son, Raymond for whom he built a house in 1957.)

In 1935, a second son, Richard John, was born. Raymond, ten years Richard's senior, watched over his little brother diligently. Because of the way Anna and Kostik had raised them, the brothers remained very close throughout their lives. Kostik was a family man dedicated to his sons as he was dedicated to his work.

He enjoyed taking the boys to work with him whenever he could. He let them sit in the back of the pickup truck, hold a rope over the truck's tailgate, and pretend they were fishing.

An incident that showed his dedication to his work occurred during a hurricane. New Jersey is frequently the target of hurricanes and 1938 was one of those target years. The 1938 hurricane was especially severe and deadly. Winds that reached 160 miles per hour created surf with waves surging to twenty-five to thirty feet high. As they came ashore, they destroyed many homes. Even the three and four-story mansions of the wealthy were not spared. For example, in one area just south of Sandy Hook in the town of Sea Bright, the ocean came ashore, crossed the spit of land and deposited itself in the Shrewsbury River, destroying a number of homes. The destruction was not confined to New Jersey. In the Northeast, the storm killed an estimated

600-800 people. Damage was estimated at $308 million, the equivalent of $4.8 billion in today's dollars. It ranked as one of the costliest hurricanes to hit the nation. Because of an increase in population and infrastructure, had the hurricane hit in the early twenty-first century, the damage would probably have been in excess of $39 billion. At the time, 4,500 farms and homes were destroying along with 26,000 automobiles and 20,000 electrical poles. In addition, an estimated 2 billion trees were flattened throughout the Northeast.

While the storm was raging, Anna and the boys were waiting for Kostik to return from a construction site where he was building a new house. When he did not return by 7:00 p.m Anna and the boys got into their heavy Buick and drove to the construction site. Anna, of course, was worried about what might have happened to Kostik. When they arrived at the building site, Anna was furious, and the boys were surprised when they saw that Kostik had his pickup truck aimed at the house with the high beams on. In spite of the howling wind and pounding rain and he was putting siding on the house. He survived the hurricane but never forgot the tongue-lashing Anna gave him. He didn't dare open his mouth to rebut her accusatory bawling out.

Fortunately, no damage was done to either their house or their garage; however, the huge weeping willow tree whose branches could completely hide a person was blown down. The whole family was sad since the tree had been a very beautiful addition to the house and yard. Unfortunately, no one checked the number of rings in its trunk, so its age was never determined.

Years after Kostik had come to America and had an established business, he was able to pursue other interests. For him it was music, for which he had talent. He was fascinated with three instruments, The violin, accordion and concertina. In the 1930's he bought one of each and taught himself to play all three. A Carnegie Hall star he was not, but he played quite well especially for one who had learned and played by ear.

His love of music extended to encouraging his sons to play. He started his son Raymond on the violin but a few years later he transitioned to trumpet. When his younger son Richard reached age five, Kostik started him on trumpet. Both boys did very well with their trumpets. In addition to music, Kostik was very hard on the boys in education. He strongly stresses the value of it strongly. To him, a "C" was a failing grade. In Russia, the Czar allowed peasants only a fourth-grade education. No such restrictions existed in America. Therefore, Kostik made sure that his sons understood from the day they were born they were going to college, no discussion. Kostik's strong stand paid off. Both boys graduated from the University of Notre Dame. Later with Kostik's love of America, his sons made him proud when they served as officers in the United States Navy.

Kostik's life was full and very rewarding. He lived to be ninety-eight years of age.

NOTE TO THE READER

Throughout this book are written conversations of Kostik Kopituk with various other people. Understand that the early conversations are all spoken in the Russian language and/or in Russian with an interpreter. As Kostik learns American (English), the conversations are in English and Russian, depending upon with whom Kostik is speaking. Conversations later in the book, as Kostik masters more of the English language, the conversations may be in English, but Kostik never loses his accent entirely.

Printed in the United States
By Bookmasters